Very Superstitious

For my Dearest Emma-Loola
Here's to another twenty years!

Disclaimer:
This book and its contents are intended for general informational and entertainment purposes only and should not be relied upon as factual or purporting to be factual or promoting a belief or encouraging any specific practice based on the information in this book. Neither the publisher nor the author is engaged in rendering factual beliefs or statements as detailed in this book. You are strongly encouraged to obtain appropriate independent professional or religious or medical advice before engaging in or relying on any of the information detailed in this book.

The publisher and the author make no representations or warranties of any kind, express or implied, with respect to the factual accuracy (both intended and purported accuracy), completeness or currency of the contents of this book, and specifically disclaim, without any limitation, any implied warranties of merchantability or fitness for a particular purpose and any injury, illness, damage, liability or loss incurred, directly or indirectly, from the use or application of any of the contents of this book. Furthermore, the publisher and the author are not affiliated with and do not sponsor or endorse any uses of or beliefs about superstitions as being religiously and or scientifically accurate or advisable in any way referred in this book.

Published in 2022 by Welbeck
An imprint of Welbeck Non-Fiction Limited,
part of Welbeck Publishing Group.
Based in London and Sydney
www.welbeckpublishing.com

Design and layout © Welbeck Non-Fiction Limited 2022
Text © Willow Winsham 2022

A CIP catalogue record for this book is available from the British Library.

ISBN 978-1-80279-501-1

Printed in Dubai

10 9 8 7 6 5 4 3 2 1

Illustrations: Suzanne Washington except pages 212, 213, 218, 219, endpapers © Julia Dreams via Creative Market

MIX
Paper | Supporting
responsible forestry
FSC
www.fsc.org
FSC® C004800

Very Superstitious

The enchanting origins
of 100 superstitions

WILLOW WINSHAM

WELBECK

CONTENTS

INTRODUCTION

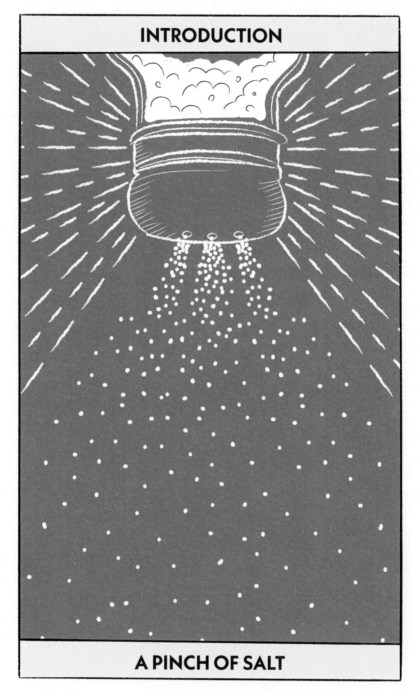

A PINCH OF SALT

What is superstition? According to the dictionary definition, a superstition is: "a belief or practice resulting from ignorance, fear of the unknown, trust in magic or chance, or a false conception of causation." Being labelled as superstitious has long-held negative connotations, often used as an insult or way to denigrate.

Although it is tempting to think of superstition as something from the uneducated past, superstitious belief permeates our lives even today. Do you knock on wood after tempting fate, or cross your fingers in the hope that something will come true? Perhaps you avoid cracks in the pavement as you walk? If so, you are not alone – these are just a few of the superstitions people carry out daily without even thinking, so ingrained are they into our collective cultural psyches.

In the pages that follow, we will embark on a whirlwind tour across time and place, looking at one hundred of the most fascinating – and in some cases, most obscure – superstitions from across the globe. Is it unlucky if a hare crosses your path? Just why should you avoid mentioning the name of one of Argentina's former presidents? When is it considered lucky to throw water over someone? Gathered from a variety of sources, from books and archives, to word of mouth and the depths of the internet, the superstitions included are just the tip of the iceberg. Through them, we not only explore what it means to be superstitious, but also discover the unifying similarities and glorious differences between superstitious beliefs across the world.

An in-depth exploration of every superstition and location is beyond the scope of this book. So, the most interesting and relevant facts about each superstition are covered, with a selection of the locations where it is found, rather than an exhaustive list. There is also a fine line between superstition and cultural tradition, for that reason, and to avoid offence or cultural appropriation, certain practices have been omitted. It must also be remembered that many superstitions in this day and age are outdated and offensive, and inclusion within this book does not equate to endorsement.

So grab a drink, sit back, and lose yourself for a while in a journey through some of the strangest and most fascinating superstitions from across the globe!

ITCHY PALMS

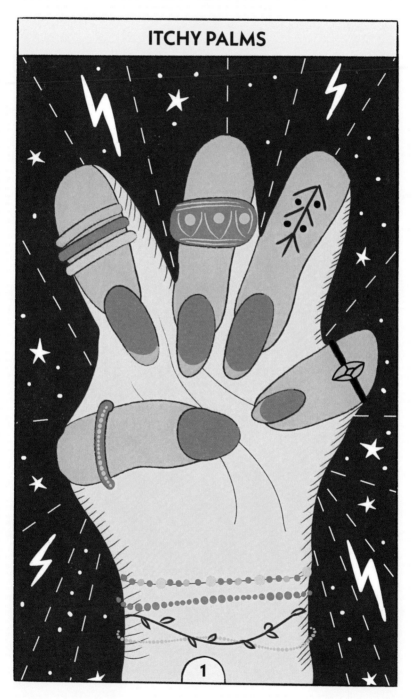

1

Have you ever felt an itching on the palm of your hand? According to belief across the world, this could be a sign that money is soon to come your way. Before you start celebrating, however, take note of which palm has the itch; some believe that an itchy left palm will bring with it a windfall, while an itchy right palm will lead to a loss of money. Others hold that the reverse is true, and that an itch on the right will bring you good fortune, but an itch on the left will lead to giving money away. Don't be too despondent if the wrong hand is itching though – popular belief states that any ill luck can be cancelled out by rubbing the afflicted palm against wood.

The belief that itchy palms are connected to money is widespread, prevalent in particular in the UK, the US, Turkey, India and Russia. It is often said that this link between palms and money stems back to a European practice in the pre-Christian era. During this time, rubbing afflicted skin with silver was believed to cure disease, and it has been suggested that, over time, itchy palms and money have thus become connected in popular culture.

It is also important how you go about scratching your itch. If you scratch the palm of your left hand with the fingers of the right, then you will be sure to lose money. The opposite, however – scratching the palm of your right hand with the fingers of your left – means that money will come your way.

There is a saying, left to leave, right to receive. This highlights the general belief that the right side of the body is inherently good, and therefore an itch anywhere on that side of the body will bring good fortune. The left side, however, is considered unlucky, and is sometimes linked to the Devil. In India, some Hindus give and receive money with the right hand, and not the left, since the right hand is associated with good and clean tasks.

LUCKY HORSESHOE

2

Horseshoes are considered to be linked to good luck – or a lack of it – across the globe. They are a familiar sight and are often found hanging over doorways and other points of access, as a sign of prosperity and protection.

There is a great deal of debate over which way to hang a horseshoe. Some swear that the shoe must be hung with the open end upwards, in order to prevent the luck from falling out. Others insist that the open end should point downwards, allowing the luck to reach those who pass beneath it.

How did horseshoes come to be such symbols of good fortune? One of the most common theories is due to horseshoes being made of iron. Iron has long been considered a form of protection against bad magic, witches and all sorts of ill-fortune, across Europe, Asia and the US.

According to one legend, the future St Dunstan, an English bishop of the tenth century, was visited in his forge by a stranger asking to be re-shoed. Spying cloven feet, the horrified Dunstan realized that his customer was the Devil himself; thinking quickly, he hid his fear and agreed to the request. He drove the nails into the soft part of the Devil's foot, causing such agony that from that day forth, it is said that the Devil would be repelled by the very sight of a horseshoe.

The number of nails a shoe is held together by can apparently influence how lucky a shoe may be. The more nails, the more luck, and often seven is considered to be the perfect number. The number of nails can also signify how many years of good luck you can expect.

In nineteenth-century Germany, there was a belief that finding a horseshoe and nailing it over a doorway, with its points facing outwards, would protect a home against witches, fire and lightning. If the points faced inwards, bad fortune would come. A belief from Bohemia, however, cautioned against picking up a horseshoe; it was thought that the person who did so would be picking up bad luck for themselves.

Horseshoes are not only considered lucky on land – sailors have been known to nail them to the masts of their ships to help avoid storms.

PASSING ON THE STAIRS

Never pass upon the stairs, you'll meet an angel unawares. Meeting someone heading in the other direction as we are walking up or down the stairs is a common occurrence, but were you aware that to cross paths with them is said to bring great misfortune?

This belief was so strongly held in nineteenth-century England that some people flat out refused to pass someone on the stairs, whatever the inconvenience. Instead, they would either return to their rooms or head back down the stairs – an action also fraught with peril – as it was considered bad luck by some to turn back whilst on the way upstairs. Obviously this could lead to problems, both if you want to avoid passing someone, but likewise if you have forgotten something on your way up. All is not lost – if you really do need to retrace your steps, whistling while doing so or walking down backwards could apparently help to counteract the bad luck.

If you really cannot avoid passing someone on the stairs, keeping your fingers crossed as you do so is hoped to stop the misfortune that could be coming your way. Holding your breath is also said to offer some protection.

From a practical perspective, passing on the stairs could lead to a dangerous fall, especially in days gone by when staircases were narrow or winding. Some believe, however, that this superstition has come about due to a connection between stairs and the way to Heaven itself, the literal stairway to Heaven. Passing on the stairs is therefore linked with death, the inevitable and final step before ascending heavenwards.

What happens if you stumble on the stairs? While tripping downwards comes with obvious danger, to trip while heading upwards is actually considered to be good luck, and is thought to lead to either your own wedding, or that of the next person to go up the stairs after you.

SALUTING MAGPIES

4

One for sorrow, two for mirth, three for a funeral, four for a birth. So goes the popular late eighteenth-century rhyme. Despite many variations of the verse over the years, in the UK and North America, the sight of a solitary magpie is well known as a sign of impending bad luck. Later additions to the rhyme include: *five for silver, six for gold, seven for a secret never to be told, eight for heaven, nine for hell.* Some rhymes go as far as thirteen! A Lancashire variant states: *five for rich, six for poor, seven for a witch.*

There are several ways to apparently negate the bad luck of seeing a lone magpie. Saluting the bird is common, as is asking after the wellbeing of himself and his wife, since alluding to the second magpie then brings on good luck. To raise your hat or blink rapidly to make one magpie appear like two is also thought to help, as is flapping your arms and squawking like a second magpie. Spitting three times over your shoulder or turning around three times is also suggested. According to Somerset lore, simply carry an onion with you at all times and you should be well protected.

Magpies are not considered to be bad luck throughout the world. In Mongolia, magpies are said to control the weather, and in China, a singing magpie is a sign of happiness and good fortune. In Korea, magpies are also thought to bring good luck, and it is the crow that signifies bad luck.

Magpies certainly have a bad reputation. According to legend, the magpie has a drop of the Devil's blood underneath its tongue. The magpie bears the stigma of apparently being the only bird to refrain from crying during the crucifixion, choosing to offer no comfort to the suffering Christ. It was also said to have eschewed the refuge of Noah's ark, instead sitting outside swearing and chattering throughout the storm. Particularly in England, France and Italy, the magpie is known as a thief of shiny objects and as a scavenger, linked to death and suffering.

BREAKING EGGSHELLS

5

Are you fond of a couple of boiled eggs for breakfast? According to popular superstition, it is a good idea to break the shells up before disposing of them. If not, you run the risk of witches using them for their nefarious purposes.

This was a commonly held belief across the UK, but there were some variations from area to area. In nineteenth-century Pembrokeshire, Wales, witches were said to have settled from Flanders (now part of Belgium) many years before, apparently using eggshell boats to make their journey. These witches were to be greatly feared, and it was considered important to crush your eggshells to prevent them from harming both the people eating the eggs and the hens that laid them.

In Ireland, pushing a spoon through the bottom of an eggshell after eating was encouraged, again to prevent witches from using them as ships and also bringing bad fortune to the egg-eater. In Ireland and Scotland, another variation was to break the shell in the shape of a cross in order to deter witches. According to Breton belief, an eggshell should be broken by striking it three times to prevent someone placing a curse on you.

English MP Reginald Scott references the belief in his 1584 *Discoverie of Witches*, where he mentions witches sailing in eggshells. During the witch trials of the sixteenth and seventeenth centuries, witches were often accused of raising storms and causing danger and death to sailors and seamen. It made sense, therefore, to prevent them from taking to the water to carry out their schemes.

It was not only witches who might use eggshells for evil purposes. In Ireland, it was thought that fairies often frequented unbroken shells. In the Netherlands, elves were believed to use eggshells as boats. Russian water spirits were also sometimes said to use eggshells as a mode of transport. In Portugal, it is advised that eggshells are broken as quickly as possible due to the Devil living in them.

The belief that eggshells should be broken to avoid being spellbound or harmed by evil magic was recorded as early as the first century CE, when Roman author Pliny the Elder referred to the practice as widespread.

CHEWING GUM AT NIGHT

6

Chewing gum is controversial at the best of times; some people love it, while others think that to chew gum is the height of rudeness. Most are agreed that it's really annoying to tread in gum and have it all over your shoe. A superstition held in Turkey, however, takes the gum debate to a whole new level. According to this belief, you should never, ever chew gum at night. Why not? Because anyone who does so is said to actually be chewing the flesh of the dead!

While this superstition seems to be particular to Turkey, there are other beliefs linked to eating after the sun has gone down, and in many parts of the world it is said to be a bad idea. Eating in the dark is often frowned upon, as it is said that you are inviting the dead to eat with you – if this weren't spooky enough, it could also lead to illness or even death. In Tanzania, eating in the dark is said to be eating with the Devil. Not only that, but be really careful if you drink at night time; it is said that if the cup you have drunk from is left uncovered, there is a chance that your soul will leap into it. If someone else then covers it, you will apparently die immediately. Ugandan belief also suggests that eating in the dark is to eat with demons, and bad luck could follow.

Another popular belief is that eating cheese before bed will bring strange dreams and poor sleep, while in South Korea, it is believed that eating apples late at night will bring on indigestion and a bad night's sleep. It is also commonly thought that eating at night will lead to weight gain. Between demons, death, general bad luck and piling on the pounds, is it worth risking it?

TOASTING WITH WATER

7

Drinking a toast is a well-known part of celebrations and commemorative gatherings, from birthdays to weddings and everything in between. It might come as a surprise, however, to learn that according to superstition, *what* you sip from your glass is actually important, and that toasting with water is believed to come with some dire consequences.

According to the US Navy's *Mess Night Manual*, toasting with water is a big no-no. To toast with water is said to lead to death by drowning and a watery grave for the person being toasted. Liquor and soft drinks of any kind are also avoided for a toast: stick to the standard champagne and wine to be on the safe side.

The same source suggests a creative origin for this particular superstition. When political and military leader Oliver Cromwell was ruling England after the execution of Charles I, the successor to the throne, James II, was in exile on the Continent. Those in the British military loyal to the crown were said to pass their wine over their water goblets in a surreptitious gesture of loyalty to the "king over the water", a secret signal and homage to the absent exile. It is said that upon discovery of this practice, water glasses were supposedly removed before wine or port was brought out, a practice continued until this day in the navy.

Another popular belief is that this taboo against a watery toast stems back to Ancient Greece. People would toast departed loved ones with water, to symbolize their drinking from the River Lethe in the underworld. Toasting with water therefore could be wishing death on the person you have toasted or on yourself.

Toasting with water or another non-alcoholic beverage is avoided in Spain with good cause; it is believed that such a toast will lead to seven years of bad luck in the bedroom department! This is also said to be the consequence in Germany and France if you break eye contact with the person you are toasting – it might be better to just avoid toasting at all!

NEW SHOES ON THE TABLE

8

A prevalent and widespread belief throughout much of the UK is that you should not, under any circumstances, place new shoes or boots on a table.

What might happen if you are careless about where you put your new shoes? It might lead to anything from an argument to a death in the family. In Orkney, Scotland, it was believed that shoes on the table would lead to thunder and lightning.

There are many – unproven – theories regarding the origin of this particular superstition. The most pragmatic explanation is simply that it was undesirable to have muddy boots on a clean table, but this doesn't account for the fact that it is specifically *new* – and therefore clean – shoes that are to be kept well away from the tabletop.

Some theories say that the taboo stems from the practice of laying out a corpse – fully dressed – for a wake. Another, more grisly, theory is the link between shoes and the gallows. It was said that when a hangman had done his job and the noose was loosened, the shoes of the hanged person would tap against the platform of the gallows. Shoes on the table were supposed to be an unwelcome and unlucky reminder of this.

An alternative theory suggests that it was common to commemorate the death of a miner by placing his boots upon the table, and that this is why putting shoes on a table is so frowned upon.

Placing shoes on a table is also a taboo in theatre circles, with the belief that it might lead to a quarrel or the actor stuttering on stage. Putting shoes on a shelf is seen to be even worse as it suggests that the actor might find his own feet raised; either by a fall or perhaps death.

If new shoes do accidentally get placed upon a table, it is said that the bad luck can be undone by spitting on the soles of the shoes in question, knocking on wood or throwing salt over your shoulder.

PICKING UP PENNIES

9

Find a penny, pick it up. All day long, you'll have good luck. There are few in the UK and the US who have not heard this popular rhyme, and it is highly likely that you will have uttered the words at least in your head when finding a penny on the ground. It is believed that this popular rhyme came from a much older one referring to pins: *See a pin and pick it up, all day long you'll have good luck. See a pin and let it lie, you'll feel want before you die.*

However, be aware that finding a coin at the start of the day is thought to come as a warning. A penny found in the morning might mean you lose more money that day! If you do pick up a penny, make sure it hasn't been discarded by someone else. Superstition holds that throwing a penny over your shoulder will remove bad luck from a person, but at the expense of the one who picks it up. It is good luck to find a coin at the racetrack, but only pick it up if it is facing heads up. If it is facing tails, the penny will bring you bad luck. Some go so far as to say that it is bad luck to *not* pick up a coin if you find it. The luckiest coin of all is considered to be one from the year of your birth: if you find one, keep it with you.

The luck of a penny, however, is not restricted to picking one up: pennies are popular good luck charms. Many people carry them in the belief that they will improve their fortunes. Some suggest that rubbing a penny over a wart for nine mornings in a row will remove it. Others believe that being in possession of a penny will stop witches from riding you (causing sleep paralysis). Throwing a penny over your left shoulder will apparently even improve your luck when losing at cards!

So common is the belief in the good luck of the penny, that there is even Lucky Penny Day in the US, celebrated on 23 May each year.

SPILLING SALT

10

For much of history, salt has been one of the most treasured commodities known to humankind. The spilling of it was considered a terrible thing, a fact still reflected in superstitions today.

Generally, spilt salt was said to herald an argument, as salt was linked to friendship due to its symbolic purity and incorruptibility. In Russia, the spilling of salt is thought to mean that family members will soon be bickering. A German saying "whoever spills salt arouses enmity" speaks of a similar belief. In the UK, spilt salt was also often linked to anger and arguments and thus discord between friends or family. Throwing some over your shoulder – usually the left shoulder – or casting some of the spilt salt into the fire could apparently hope to undo at least a little of the bad luck to come. Some believe that it should be specifically the right hand that tosses the salt. It is also sometimes said that it is important to remain silent until the whole process has been carried out. Spilling salt is also sometimes thought to indicate that a broken bone is on the cards.

Norwegian belief holds that the amount of salt spilt is important; the more that is spilt, the more tears will be shed in order to dissolve the lost salt. Some say that a tear will be shed for every grain of salt that has been dropped.

Throwing salt over the left shoulder had a practical purpose; the Devil was said to hover there, and throwing salt into his eyes would divert him from causing any further harm. Salt has been used by many cultures in protection against witches, demons or bad spirits due to its divine connections, and is therefore said to be greatly reviled by the Devil.

Leonardo Da Vinci's depiction of Judas upending the salt cellar in *The Last Supper* is believed to have added to the negative connotations of a salt spillage, due to his betrayal of Christ and the subsequent crucifixion.

WEARING CLOTHES INSIDE OUT

11

We've all done it; got dressed in a hurry, only to realize that we've put on an item of clothing inside out. Although easily solved, don't be so quick to rectify the mistake, as it could have untoward consequences on the rest of your day.

In England during the sixteenth century, inside out clothing was known as a possible cause of bad luck. From the mid-eighteenth century onwards, however, there is evidence of the belief that the inside-out garment would bring good luck – as long as the clothing was not returned to its proper state. If this was done, then the good luck would also be reversed. It was only good luck though if the item was inside out by accident.

In Yorkshire, the practice of "smock turning" took place, where women turned their shirts inside out to ensure a fair wind for their loved ones at sea. Some items were luckier than others; an inside-out stocking, for instance, was considered luckier than a petticoat or a waistcoat.

In Ireland, putting a stocking on inside out was considered lucky. There is a widespread belief that the item needs to stay inside out until undressing at night. The belief in China also states that to turn the clothing the right way again will undo the good luck. In Cyprus, the belief is the opposite, that wearing clothing inside out will mean your day goes contrary to how you want it to. Egyptian belief likewise suggests that the day would be turned inside out, with you sleeping all day and awake all night.

Wearing clothes inside out was also thought to mean that you would see a stranger, or, in the very specific case of putting a right stocking on inside out on a Monday morning, you would attract a present.

Inside-out pyjamas are often used, especially by children in the US, as a ritual for invoking snowfall, in the belief that wearing them inside out and/or backwards will bring much wanted snow.

Wearing clothing inside out intentionally was also said to protect someone from being led astray by pixies or fairies.

WHITE RABBITS

12

Beginnings are important, and none more so than that which marks the fresh start of a new month. One way to ensure that the weeks to follow go well, according to common superstition in the US, the UK, Australia and New Zealand, is to utter the words "Rabbit, rabbit, rabbit".

There are various variations; "white rabbits" or "white rabbit" or just a single "rabbit" is preferred by some. Be careful though; for the words to work, some say they must be the first thing you say that day. Similarly, any good effect will be lost if rashly uttered after midday on the first of the month. Some people believe that the speaker will receive a gift in return, along with a month of good fortune.

No one really knows the origin of these sayings, although "rabbits" was attested to in at least the early twentieth century in the UK. It is also said that American President Franklin Roosevelt admitted to following this superstition, and never neglected to say "rabbits" on the first day of the month. He was also thought to carry a rabbit's foot in his pocket for good luck.

A connected and equally popular phrase is to say: "pinch, punch, first day of the month." This is accompanied by the relevant actions, and a hasty "and no returns" or "white rabbit", which protects the pincher from being pinched and punched in return. Those who aren't quick enough, however, run the risk of the pinched retaliating with "a flick and a kick for being so quick"! Some believe that the pinch refers to a pinch of salt to stop a witch, and the punch to send her away.

Again, variations of exact phrasing occur, with added retorts. For instance, in New Zealand, "a kick in the toe for being so slow", means that the exchange can continue for quite some time. Needless to say, this superstition is one that children are particularly fond of, and both "rabbits" and "pinch punch" are still very much in practice today.

EATING 12 GRAPES ON NEW YEAR'S EVE

13

According to Spanish tradition, on *Nochevieja* – "Old Night", or New Year's Eve – in order to guarantee good fortune for the year ahead, you need to join in with a country-wide ritual. As the clock strikes 12 to herald in the New Year, 12 grapes must be eaten, one for each chime. Not only that, they must be completely consumed by the time the chimes finish – no mean feat, and a challenge that often leads to much hilarity and competition.

Eating these 12 lucky grapes – *las doce uvas de la suerte* – has been a tradition since at least 1909. Some say that this was when the superstition first took off due to an overabundant grape crop that year in Alicante and some savvy thinking by vineyard owners. There is evidence, however, that this just popularized an existing tradition from the late nineteenth century.

Each grape symbolizes one month: a sour grape and the month will likewise be sour; sweet and expect good fortune that month. If you don't manage to eat all of your grapes before the end of that final chime, beware, as bad luck awaits. Some maintain that an item of red underwear must be worn to ensure good luck.

Aledo grapes are the most frequently used, pale in colour, with extra thin skins, perfect for fast chewing and swallowing. The tradition is so popular that you can now buy cans of 12 seedless, peeled grapes in Spanish supermarkets ready for the big day.

The superstition has spread over recent years, and has also become popular in some areas of Central and South America. In Mexico, 12 grapes are also eaten: these either represent the 12 months, or a wish is made with each grape, and if you eat all of them, your wishes are said to come true. A variation is using 12 round fruits, with each person taking a bite of each fruit before the chimes end.

Beware though: if you start eating that first grape too early, before the first chime, then you can look forward to a year of bad luck ahead.

BREAKING A MIRROR

14

An almost universal superstition is the belief that breaking a mirror will lead to great calamity. In many instances, the outcome is unequivocal; to break a mirror means a death will soon follow in the family. Some believe, instead, that the breakage will lead to the loss of a friendship, another undesirable, although less final, consequence.

In Russia, breaking a mirror is thought to herald great misfortune for a friend. Under no circumstances should you look at yourself in a broken mirror, a belief also held in India and elsewhere. Many cultures throughout history have believed that a mirror holds the soul of the person reflected there. It stands to reason therefore that if the glass becomes harmed in any way, the soul would be likewise affected.

Although often linked to the Roman belief that the human body renewed itself every seven years, the popular idea that to break a mirror brings with it seven years of bad luck was only first attested in print in England in the mid-nineteenth century. In Italy, there is also the belief that breaking a mirror brings seven years of bad luck.

If you do break a mirror, don't be tempted to keep the broken shards, since to do so will only magnify the bad luck to come. Instead, try burying the broken pieces by the light of the full moon or grinding them into dust in an attempt to ward off the bad luck.

This superstition does not just extend to humans. In mid-nineteenth century England, it was said that if a cat broke a mirror, another cat in the household would pay the price.

If you break a mirror during Chinese New Year, misfortune can apparently be avoided if you gather up the pieces and wrap them in red cloth or paper, before throwing them into a lake or river on the fifth day.

Some think that the size of the mirror matters; breaking a small one is said to bring fewer years of bad luck than breaking a larger one. If you drop a mirror and it doesn't break, breathe a sigh of relief: good luck is coming your way!

13

If there is one day on which to take extra care when doing anything, it is said to be Friday 13th. Indeed, the fear of this specific date is so pervasive in some areas of the Western world that there is a term for it: paraskevidekatriaphobia.

In the US, it is estimated that over 80 per cent of high rise buildings are without a 13th floor, a trend that is also reflected in room numbers in hospitals and hotels. In the UK, some roads and estates are without a 13th house, likewise reflecting this taboo, whereas governing bodies in Edinburgh, Scotland and Vancouver, Canada, disapprove of this practice and refuse to allow the omission.

Although Friday and the number 13 have been reviled separately for centuries, it was only in the mid-nineteenth century that the two became conflated into the epitome of misfortune it is known as today. Origins include Norse myth, where the god of mischief Loki gate-crashed a dinner at Valhalla to become the 13th guest. And it proved unlucky indeed, as chaos, death and sadness swiftly ensued. Other reinforcements of this link include the Christian belief of the Last Supper on Good Friday, where Judas (who betrayed Jesus) made up the 13th disciple, and the fact that the Christian military order of the Knights Templar were arrested on a Friday 13th, in 1307.

Germany and New Zealand are among other countries where Friday 13th is considered unlucky. In Spain, Tuesday 13th, *martes trece*, is best avoided, and Tuesday 13th is also avoided in Greece, partly due to the association with the fall of Constantinople on that date in 1204. In Italy, it is Friday 17th that is considered inauspicious. Thirteen was actually considered lucky in Ancient Egypt, and the number is seen as lucky in Italy today.

Are you actually more likely to run into bother when the 13th day of the month falls on a Friday? Some studies show an increase in accidents on the roads on those days, but others show the reverse: that, due to people avoiding going out, and being more careful if they do, the roads are actually marginally safer! And some good news: Friday 13th only occurs between one and three times each calendar year; it could be worse!

OPENING AN UMBRELLA INDOORS

16

On a rainy day, chances are you'll be reaching for your umbrella. If you are ever tempted to open your brolly before stepping out into the elements, however, or stand it open in the hallway to dry, it might be time to think again, as opening an umbrella indoors is believed by many to bring bad luck.

Some suggest that the superstition has an ancient heritage. In Ancient Egypt, it was believed that opening a sun parasol indoors was disrespectful to the sun god, Ra, and would anger him. It is also thought that opening an umbrella inside angers household spirits, as you are rejecting the protection they offer.

It was only in the latter half of the nineteenth century that umbrellas became used to protect people from rain, and most of the evidence for this superstition in the UK dates from the Victorian era onwards. Operated with a vicious spring mechanism, the force was violent enough to cause damage to a person or property. Because of this association with bad luck and also perhaps as a deterrent, the superstition took hold that it was unlucky to open one indoors.

It is thought that opening an umbrella indoors could bring general bad luck, an argument or rain. If opening the umbrella indoors wasn't bad enough, holding it over your head is thought to herald certain disaster – many believe that to do so means a death will occur. An umbrella hung with the opening upwards is also risky: opportunistic pixies might take up residence there, ready to spill out when you open it. In areas of France, it is frowned upon to leave an umbrella open to dry in the house, so be sure to close it instead. Some say it is unlucky to place an umbrella on a bed as it is said to be inviting disease or even death into the house.

If you open an umbrella outside when the weather is fine, it is thought that you are in danger of inviting rain. Carrying one unopened, however, is apparently a good method of keeping rain away!

SPILLING WINE

17

A nice glass of wine is a popular choice of drink for many, either at home or when out for a meal with friends. By their very design, a wine glass is prone to toppling, and however careful we are, accidents can and do happen. What does this mean in terms of our fortunes?

Spilling wine is generally considered to be bad luck in many cultures. According to belief in ancient Rome, to accidentally spill wine was considered an omen of great disaster to come. Likewise today in Italy, the accidental spilling of wine – whether on the table or on the floor – is considered to be bad luck, beyond the obvious loss of a good drink. Even the slightest spill could lead to unwanted negative consequences. There is an antidote, however: if you do happen to spill some of your drink, just dab a little of the spilled wine behind each ear – some say specifically with the middle finger of your right hand – and all will, hopefully, be well!

Intentionally spilling wine, however, is often seen as a good omen. Pouring wine onto the deck of a ship is said to ensure good luck for the voyage ahead. The breaking of a glass filled with wine at a wedding is likewise believed to bring good luck, and a long and happy marriage filled with love for the couple. In the seventeenth century, purposefully spilling wine into someone's lap was also seen as an antidote to the bad luck attracted when salt was spilt in their direction.

Spilt wine could also serve other purposes, and in the sixteenth and seventeenth centuries was a well-known method of divination to foresee future events. The spilling of other drinks was also said to influence luck: according to seventeenth-century English belief, to have drink spilled on a person was seen as good fortune, as was beer being spilt near you.

KNOCKING ON WOOD

18

The practice of touching or knocking on wood to avert bad luck can be found the world over. It is most often carried out after someone has uttered a rashly optimistic statement – such as saying something bad hasn't happened yet – or when discussing future plans, and knocking on wood is said to stop the bad thing from happening. In the UK and Australia, people "touch wood" whereas the majority of other countries "knock on wood".

One suggested origin of this superstition is that of knocking on trees to ask for the protection of the wood sprites that were said to dwell within. Another is that it stems from the association of good luck when touching remnants from Christ's wooden cross. Another theory in the UK links to a child's game of tig-touch-wood – a version of tag where to be touching wood meant you couldn't be caught.

The number of times to touch or knock on wood varies. In many places, one knock is sufficient. In Georgia, Portugal and Brazil, it is three knocks. In County Clare, Ireland, two knocks were deemed sufficient. In Denmark, people knock three times under the table, saying *syv-ni-tretten* – seven – nine – thirteen – saying one number with each knock. In Sweden, it is best to say *Peppar, peppar tai tra*, or "Pepper, pepper, knock on wood," to guarantee that bad luck will be averted.

The type of wood could also be important. Some knock on any wooden surface, while others insist it has to be plain, free from paint or varnish in order to be effective. In some areas of Latin America, Bulgaria and other places, the wood must not have legs. Some believe that you should touch the table top, others that you must knock underneath it.

In Russia, knocking alone isn't enough, and often spitting three times over the left shoulder after knocking is considered necessary. In Malaysia, you should knock on wood and then on your forehead, while saying the words *tak cun tak cun*.

In an ironic, self deprecating twist, some people will touch their own head when no wood is present.

CUTTING CAKE

19

Who doesn't like a good slice of cake? Many of us enjoy tucking into a tasty treat, but far fewer are aware that, according to superstition, cutting a piece of cake can be fraught with danger.

According to Scandinavian lore, you're in for trouble if your slice of cake falls on its side while being cut or served to you. In Sweden, if this happens you should prepare for life as an old maid, as you will never marry. Conversely, in Denmark, a toppled slice means you will find yourself with a problematic mother-in-law. Perhaps the Swedish belief doesn't look so bad now! Belief that falling cake is bad luck exists in other places too, and some suggest that the bad luck can be countered by uttering the words "bread and butter."

While you should be careful with cake in general, cake for specific occasions brings with it even more room for error. For a birthday, the birthday person must make the first cut, making a wish beforehand. In Lebanon and Jordan, a wish is made while cutting the cake: but you must remember to do so with the wrong side of the knife. Elsewhere, when cutting the birthday cake, don't cut through to the bottom; this will apparently ensure you never marry. Some people avoid cutting a cake all the way across, believing that it is a surefire way to invite bad luck into your life.

Where wedding cake is concerned, the bride should be the first person to cut the cake to ensure prosperity and happiness throughout life. The knife should be upside down and not the right way up. Also beware – it is said that it is bad luck to cut the top tier of a wedding cake at all before the couple's first anniversary.

When baking a batch of small cakes, don't eat them all at once. The first one to come out of the oven should be carefully broken open to ensure the quality of any other cakes baked the same day. If the cake is rashly cut instead, then it is thought that all further cakes will be soggy.

SEEING YOUR DOPPELGANGER

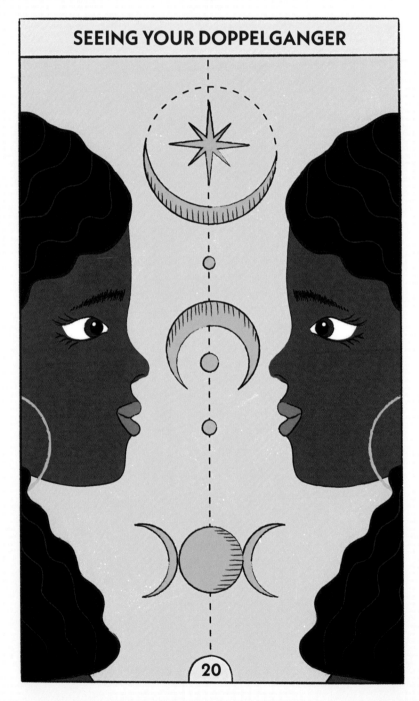

20

There is a belief that everyone has a spirit double, an exact replica of themselves. This doppelganger, or double goer, is greatly feared in England and Germany, where it is said that to see one's own doppelganger is an omen of death. If someone else witnesses your doppelganger, then you should take heed, as it suggests that you might soon fall ill.

The term was coined in the late eighteenth century, but belief in the spirit duplicate existed long before that. In Norse belief there was the *vardøger*. This form carries out a person's actions before they do it themselves, and those who witness the *vardøger* relate hearing or seeing a person before they have actually arrived – a bizarre kind of reverse déjà-vu. Then there is the *ka* of Egyptian mythology; this was believed to be a part of the soul, identical to the person in question.

In the southern states of the US and other areas, it is believed that the more times you meet your doppelganger, the worse the outcome. Three sightings were supposed to be particularly ominous, with many accounts of death occurring after the third.

One of the most famous accounts of a doppelganger sighting involves the former American president Abraham Lincoln. Lincoln told his wife that he had witnessed two reflections when he looked in the mirror, one that looked much paler than his own physical form. He saw his double again on two subsequent occasions, a fact that led his wife to believe that Lincoln would die before his second term of office was at an end. This did indeed come true: he was assassinated part way through his second term.

Catherine the Great, Elizabeth I and poet Percy Bysshe Shelley are all also said to have seen their doppelgangers before their deaths, so if you happen to see your spirit double, you are at least in good historical company!

STICKING CHOPSTICKS INTO RICE

21

Chopsticks are for eating with, and it makes perfect sense to stick them into your food when you want to take a break, right? Wrong! In many East Asian countries, and areas of the world with large Asian communities, to stick your chopsticks upright in your rice is deeply frowned upon.

There are several reasons for this taboo. In China, a bowl of rice with chopsticks in was often placed on a grave or an ancestral shrine as an offering, in case the dead grew hungry. By doing so at your meal, you might inadvertently cause offence to, or even summon, the dead to your table, literally offering food to the dead. Similarly, in Japan, in both Shinto and Buddhist practice, at a funeral, a bowl of rice with chopsticks is offered to the spirit of the dead, likewise linking rice and chopsticks with death.

Then there is also the practice of placing incense sticks on a funeral altar to mourn those who have departed. Chopsticks in a bowl look very similar, and so it is thought by some that this recreation of a sacred ritual shows disrespect to the deceased and invites bad luck.

In Japan, don't rest your chopsticks upright in anything at all. Some say that the image resembles the number "4", which means death. In some areas, this has extended to a flat-out taboo on leaving any utensils standing in any food whatsoever.

Another thing to watch out for is making sure you keep your chopsticks in their proper pairs. In China, things that come in pairs must stay in pairs, or else you risk bad luck descending upon you and your loved ones. It is also considered bad luck to drop your chopsticks on the floor. And certainly don't play with your chopsticks at the table: it's not bad luck, but it is bad manners.

WALKING UNDER LADDERS

22

Have you ever seen a ladder and been faced with the dilemma of whether to walk under it or go out of your way to walk round it? If you have, it's likely you are one of many people the world over recalling the superstition that to walk under a ladder is to invite bad luck. In fact, some believe that to look through or pass anything through a ladder at all is just asking for trouble.

It is thought that walking under a ladder could lead to the offender never marrying or, even worse, could lead to death, perhaps at the end of a noose. Why though is walking under a ladder seen as so unlucky? There are several suggested origins for this superstition.

Some believe that this superstition stems back to Ancient Egypt, where the triangle was a symbol of life and the gods. Walking under a ladder – which makes a triangle when leaning against something – might lead to a glimpse of a god passing up or down, which would anger them and bring their wrath down upon you.

Then there is the connection with the Christian Trinity; walking under the ladder again breaks the holy triangle, a most blasphemous act that must come with repercussions. Another Christian link comes from depictions of the Crucifixion, where it was believed that a ladder rested against the cross.

Perhaps the most obvious is the link to the gallows, where the condemned climbed the ladder before swinging to their deaths. It is said that in France, on the day of their execution, the condemned would walk under the ladder – unlucky indeed!

Have you walked under a ladder? All is not lost. Apparently saying "bread and butter" can revoke the bad luck, as can walking backwards through the ladder back to your starting position. Spitting three times or over one shoulder could also help keep the bad luck away, as could keeping your fingers crossed or not speaking until you have seen a dog.

If you make a wish as you pass under a ladder, it is likely to come true. It is also thought to be good luck to climb up a ladder that has an even number of rungs.

CUTTING BREAD

23

Bread continues to be the staple of countless diets throughout the world today. With its prominent and sometimes sacred place in so many cultures, one question returns again and again – what is the best way to cut it, and what happens if you do it wrong?

According to superstition, cutting bread evenly will bring good luck, so be sure to have a steady hand when cutting. It is considered bad luck to cut a loaf of bread from both ends, as it might lead to the Devil flying over your house. Make sure your loaf is the right way up before you start to cut; upside down bread can result in bad luck such as being shipwrecked or even dying. Take note of the appearance of the bread when you cut into a loaf; if you are unlucky enough to find a large hole or air bubble, beware, as this signifies a coffin, and it is likely that a death will soon follow.

Some believe that, due to its sacred nature, you should not cut bread with a knife at all. Instead hands should be used to avoid any misfortune that might follow. Some cultures believe a cross should be cut into the top of the dough before baking to prevent the Devil from sitting on – and spoiling – your bread.

Bread-themed dreams are seen as a good sign, apparently meaning that good times are on the way. And a wish made after picking bread up is said to surely come true. Dropping bread on the floor is seen as good luck, but only if it hasn't been buttered. Dropping bread butter side down is thought to be bad luck.

According to a belief in Turkey, bread is sacred, and pieces of leftover bread should not be discarded, as to do so will bring bad luck; old bread should be eaten, or given to the birds.

SWEEPING DIRT OUT OF THE HOUSE

24

This one might come as a surprise for the house-proud, but according to superstition, it is bad luck to sweep dirt and dust out of your house. It is said that you would be sweeping the good luck away from your home, and who would want to do that?

Sweeping after dark is considered bad luck in several European countries. It is best to sweep dirt out of the back door, not the front, and certainly not before the sun comes up, since this is just asking for bad luck to enter. It is also considered unlucky to sweep a table with a broom. An unwelcome guest can apparently be kept from returning if you sweep out their room the moment they have gone.

It is also important to be careful where you sweep; if you sweep over the feet of someone who is single, they will not marry that year, or perhaps ever. If the person in question is already married, bad times might be ahead. Spitting on the broom immediately afterwards is thought to hopefully reverse any bad luck.

A belief from some parts of Africa holds that sweeping the house after dark will sweep away your wealth or blessings. Sweeping in the home should be avoided during the first three days of a mourning period, for fear of causing bad luck and offending the soul of the departed. In China, all sweeping in the house is believed best avoided for the first two days of the Chinese New Year, in the belief that to sweep at that time will be sweeping away the good luck for the year ahead.

According to a rhyme, brooms can have an impact on your relationships; "Buy a broom in May, sweep a friend away." This belief was particularly prevalent in the South of England during the nineteenth and early twentieth centuries. So strong was the taboo against broom buying in May, that many businesses complained that their broom sales were drastically down in that month. In extreme cases, this extended to brushes of all sorts, even including toothbrushes!

HEARING AN OWL AT NIGHT

25

There is no sound more haunting than the screech of an owl suddenly breaking the silence of the night. It is little wonder that these majestic creatures have been linked throughout history to the magical, the dark and the terrifying.

Although venerated in Ancient Greece for their connection to the Goddess Athena, owls quickly developed a reputation for the dark and deadly. Ovid in 15CE wrote of the "ill-boding notes" of the owl, and sources consistently refer to the cry of an owl being an omen of death, from Chaucer to Shakespeare and beyond. White or barn owls were particularly feared, and in nineteenth-century England their screech was said to herald a death. An owl seated on the roof of a house, seen near a window or appearing in your dream is said to be a sure omen of death to follow.

Welsh folklore tells of the *Aderyn y Corph* or Corpse Bird, a portent of death that calls outside the door of someone who is going to die soon. It is believed that such tales are actually referring to the cry of the "screech" or barn owl. In France, if a pregnant woman hears the cry of an owl, this means she is expecting a girl. An owl cry while a woman labours in Germany, however, is said to mean that the child will be unhappy throughout their life.

It is not only at night that you should worry if you hear an owl. According to some, witnessing or hearing an owl during the daytime is of equal bad luck, and is a sign of impending tragedy. According to Roman author Pliny the Elder in 77CE, it was a bad omen to see an owl during the day, a belief that was still prevalent in England and elsewhere in the mid-nineteenth century and beyond.

Owls are not always seen as harbingers of doom. In Germany, if you jingle coins in your pocket upon hearing an owl, it is said that the year's harvest will be good. Owls are thought to be the souls of women in aboriginal Australian belief, and are therefore considered sacred.

RETURNING HOME FOR FORGOTTEN THINGS

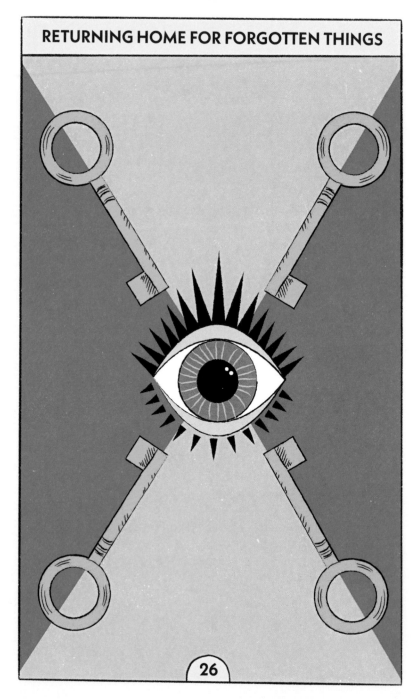

26

We've all been there. You think you've got everything you need, rush out the door, only to realize that you've left something of vital importance inside the house. The obvious thing to do is to run back in and collect it, but, according to superstition, doing so will bring on all manner of bad luck for the journey ahead.

In Romania, returning for an item is said to bring bad luck. Polish belief also dictates that doing so will put the rest of the day in peril. In Russia, returning to retrieve a forgotten item is seen as a bad omen, and if you can do without, it is best to just continue on your way. There are some things that can't be left, however, and if you do go back, make sure you look in a mirror before you leave the house again. This will apparently counter the bad luck, and make sure that your journey isn't a terrible disaster.

This superstition is likewise found in areas of the US, the UK, parts of Eastern Europe and Asia. In England, it doesn't even have to be your own house that you are leaving; leaving any house and returning for something forgotten can trigger the bad luck associated with this superstition.

There are several other ways to counter the bad luck activated by returning for a forgotten item. Of course, asking someone inside the house to bring it out to you is the first thing to try in order to avoid the problem. If this isn't an option and you do go inside, some say that smiling before leaving again will break the ill-fortune, and sitting down and resting for a specified time before setting off again is also believed to help.

TUCKING IN THUMBS WHEN WALKING
PAST A CEMETERY

27

A commonly held superstition in Japan, tucking your thumbs in when walking through or past a cemetery is considered of great importance. The words for "thumb" and "death" in Japanese sound very similar, and the thumb is also known as the parent finger. It is therefore said that to leave your thumbs out near a cemetery can lead to an early death for your parents, something most people will be keen to avoid. Holding thumbs when a hearse goes by is also practiced in Japan; if you don't, you risk not being there for your parents' funeral.

Another cemetery-related superstition popular across various parts of the world is that of holding your breath when walking past a graveyard. Some say that to do so will protect your parents. Not holding your breath for as long as you can also apparently leaves you at risk of breathing in a recently departed soul. This superstition also extends to driving, so make sure to hold your breath the next time you drive past a burial place. Some say that spirits are jealous of those still living, and breathing reminds them that you are alive while they are not. Other beliefs suggest that you are in danger of going insane or dying if you don't remember to hold your breath. The origins of this superstition are attributed to several sources, from the thirteenth-century belief that to breathe near a body that had died from plague would mean you met the same fate, to links with God breathing life – and soul – into Adam in the Bible.

It is also often considered a bad idea to point at a cemetery or a gravestone. A belief from Hawaii suggests that if you do so, a spirit might attach itself to you, and some say it will stay with you forever!

A BIRD FLYING INTO THE HOUSE

Birds feature frequently in superstitions, and a bird in the house is considered to be of great significance. Most commonly, a bird in the house is seen as a sign that a death is going to take place. In English lore, swallows were frequently cited; one flying down the chimney or into a bedroom was seen as unlucky to those who lived there. A bird flying in and then out again, or flying around the room three times, was especially dire, apparently warning that a death would happen soon. If the bird landed on the back of someone's chair, that was bad news for the person who sat there.

The colour of the bird can also be significant, with some believing that a white bird in particular signals a death in the family. If the bird dies, this is said to make the chance of a tragedy all the more likely.

In many Asian countries, however, a bird flying into the house is seen as a positive sign, suggesting prosperity and luck in the near future. Indonesian superstition states that a sparrow flying into the house is lucky, and can also mean that a wedding will soon take place. A bird in the house isn't always linked to death; it is also said to mean that news is coming soon, although this might not always be good news. In Cyprus, it is believed that a bird flying into the house means either news is to follow, or a death is to come soon.

In some cases, the bird doesn't even have to enter the home; a bird beating its wings against the window or tapping its beak is enough for some to be a harbinger of doom. Some people extend this superstition by refusing to have any pictures or symbols of birds within their homes for fear of welcoming bad luck. American actress Lucille Ball (1911–89), for instance, was said to be terrified of birds after her father died shortly after a bird entered the house. Even in adulthood, she refused to stay in hotels with pictures of birds, and ripped out silk wallpaper that had birds on it from her home.

BREAK A LEG

29

Imagine the scene – the curtain is about to go up, the cast is buzzing with anticipation and the long hours of hard work are about to pay off. Then, suddenly, someone utters the dreaded words "good luck".

Unlike in most other walks of life, wishing someone "good luck" in the theatre is akin to ensuring their entire performance is an unmitigated disaster. If you do want to wish someone well, you should tell them to "break a leg" instead.

First appearing in a theatre context in the 1920s and 1930s, the phrase "break a leg" is well known throughout the UK and the US. "Good luck" is likewise avoided in Norway where it is believed to jinx the recipient, so *tvi tvi* is used instead. This phrase sounds a bit like you are spitting, and traditionally spitting was used to ward off evil.

A dance variation, originating in France, is to utter *merde* (shit) before someone goes on stage, in the hope of a full audience; the Spanish version is *mucha mierda*, conveying the same principle. What does excrement have to do with luck? It is said to stem from nineteenth-century Paris and the days of carriage travel, when the amount of horse dung left on the street after a performance was an indication of how successful, or otherwise, a production had been.

In Australia, a cry of "chookas!" is often exchanged between performers before the curtain goes up. Some say it is derived from "chook it is!" and thus chicken for the post-performance meal, or from the more mundane "cheers and good wishes".

"Break a leg" is not thought to have originated in the theatre at all, instead having its origins in a general German phrase, *Hals und Beinbruch* – "neck and leg break". This, in turn, comes from a Yiddish saying that means success and blessing. Although this is the generally accepted version, there are other, implausible, origins, ranging from the noise made by a satisfied audience banging their feet or chair legs, to English actor David Garrick (1717–79) performing with a broken limb in the eighteenth century. Another unsubstantiated claim alludes to a performer "breaking" or crossing the leg line (a specific line on the stage) as they gained the opportunity to have paid work on the stage.

PUTTING A HAT ON YOUR BED

30

You've taken off your hat: now, where is the best place to put it? Wherever you choose to set it down, superstition holds that one place you should definitely avoid is on a bed.

The belief that to put a hat on a bed brings bad luck can be found across several disparate cultural groups. One of the earliest recorded instances is from Jamaican folklore of the late nineteenth century, when a hat on the bed was said to bring bad luck. Furthermore, if a single man did so, it was thought that he would not marry.

Sometimes the positioning of the hat was important. In early twentieth-century Illinois, US, it was recorded that it was bad luck to place a hat on a bed unless the crown was against the covers. Yet others believed that to lay the hat down crown first would actually court bad luck. To some, simply putting the hat on the bed at all would bring bad luck to whoever slept there.

A hat on the bed is frowned upon in the world of the theatre, and is considered to bring bad luck to those on the stage. Putting a hat on the bed could also lead to arguments between friends, another reason it should be avoided. Cowboys, in particular, believe strongly in this superstition, and are keen to put their hats elsewhere to avoid inviting any bad luck their way. Some believe it could even lead to injury or death.

Some say that this superstition can be traced back to the gangsters of the 1920s in the US. It is said that rival gangs would meet in a hotel room, and, for safety purposes, every man would be searched as they entered. The first to arrive, however, would set their hats on the bed and gain an advantage by concealing their weapons underneath.

A practical, alternative explanation for this superstition is that it stems from the fact that to lay a hat on a bed could lead to the spread of head lice.

SALT IN A NEW HOME

31

According to superstition across the world, if you are moving to a new house, salt should play a vital part in your moving day plans. Long known for its purifying properties, sprinkling or taking salt into a new home is believed in many places to bring protection and prosperity to the family for years to come.

In the UK, placing salt on the stairs, in the corners of the house and in the hearth would ensure good luck to the home. Some say that salt should be the first thing brought into the house, and carrying salt across the threshold or guests bringing salt as a gift is also said to have the same effect. An early twentieth-century source from Tenby, Wales records a moving man flinging salt about a house before bringing any furniture in, and a mother placing salt on the stairs, both for good luck.

According to Jewish tradition in Russia, salt and bread should be the first things taken into a house: salt to add flavour to life, and bread to make sure no one goes hungry. This belief is widespread – in India, salt and bread are likewise carried into a new house, and sprinkling salt by windows and doors is said to protect a house from evil spirits. Don't forget to hoover it up again though after a day has passed – this will ensure that anything bad is hoovered away! In the Philippines, coins are scattered in the new living room on moving day instead.

Don't take your old salt with you to your new home; leave it behind and buy fresh salt for the new home to ensure good luck will be yours.

Before you move, do check the weather; according to Icelandic belief, if it is raining on moving day you will have a prosperous life in your new home. Some, however, say the reverse, and that moving plans should be cancelled if rain threatens.

STEPPING OVER SOMEONE

32

Have you ever been in the situation where someone is sitting on the floor, legs spread out, between you and where you need to be? The easiest and quickest thing to do is to carefully step over them, with a murmured "excuse me" for good measure. Next time this occurs, however, you may want to reconsider, as in some areas of the world it is considered very unlucky to step over another person in such a manner.

In Greece, and in American families of Greek descent, it is well known that it is unlucky to step over someone who is sitting or lying down. Nothing will happen to you, the stepper, but it is believed that the person you have stepped over will have to live with the terrible consequences. Their growth will apparently be stunted, and they will remain the height they were at the time you stepped over them. If they are a fully grown adult, then some might think that this is no big issue, but others are of the firm belief that it is still best avoided.

This is also a superstition held in Russia, where it is likewise considered bad form to step over someone on the ground or floor. If you do make such a mistake, it can be undone if you act quickly. Simply step backwards over the person and then make sure not to step over them again as you go on your way.

What is the origin of this superstition? It is likely to be rooted in the idea that some believe that to step over someone is rude, and the superstition has grown to support and reinforce this social rule.

Also, be aware that stepping over any part of their body still counts – in a crowded space, you might be better off just asking someone – politely – to move!

WHISTLING AT NIGHT

Whistling is fun to do, but not always so nice to listen to. You might want to think twice, however, the next time you feel like whistling a jaunty tune, as if you happen to be whistling after dark, you might find yourself with more trouble than you bargained for.

According to many cultures, whistling at night can lead to bad fortune and the summoning of spirits. In Korean and Chinese belief, whistling at night is thought to call ghosts to follow you. In Nigeria, whistling at night is also said to summon evil spirits, something that is obviously best avoided! Similarly, in Turkey, night-time whistling is said to be calling up the Devil himself. Japanese superstition states that whistling at night will summon a snake to you – either a literal snake, or a person of undesirable character. You might also find yourself abducted by a Tengu, a terrible demon. On the other hand, whistling at night while passing a cemetery could actually have a beneficial effect, by keeping away ghosts and witches.

The fishermen of St. Ives, Cornwall, England, were known to consider whistling at night to be one of the worst sins imaginable. Whistling at sea was generally frowned upon, in case of summoning a terrible storm. In that vein, whistling when a storm was already in progress was the last thing you should do, for fear of bringing death and destruction all round.

To counteract any ill attracted by whistling at night, an early seventeenth-century antidote suggests that walking around the house three times will be penance enough to undo the bad fortune.

Whatever time of day, it has been said that it is unlucky for a woman to whistle, for she is communicating with the Devil. Likewise, whistling indoors is generally held to be a bad thing, and in Slavic cultures is said to lead a person to poverty and financial hardship.

Conversely, whistling first thing in the morning is, according to many, good luck, and will bring good fortune your way.

STEPPING ON PAVEMENT CRACKS

34

"Step on a crack, break your mother's back", or so cautions this well-known rhyme. Children and adults alike know better than to risk stepping on cracks between paving stones, for fear of untold horrors being unleashed. Another, lesser-known variation is: "step on a line, break your father's spine", carrying the same warning that to step on cracks is to bring pain and suffering to your family.

Some go further still and say that the number of lines or cracks that a person treads on counts towards the overall outcome. It is thought that for each crack or line, the unfortunate parent will break another bone, the final outcome calculated by how many cracks have been trodden on during the journey.

Some versions of this superstition involve belief in harm befalling the person themselves: many a child has skipped diligently over cracks on the walk to school, having been warned that bears or crocodiles will get them. There are other variations of this superstition that follow the same basic format, with the idea that stepping on something will have a negative consequence, such as "step on a hole, break your mother's sugar bowl".

Why are cracks seen so negatively? Some say that there is a link between cracks and the underworld, and that by treading on them you run the risk of inviting a demon into your life. Or worse, who is to say that you might not fall through the crack itself into the hellish world below?

This particular superstition is alive and well today, and a recent survey in Great Britain revealed that one in twenty respondents wouldn't tread on pavement cracks, even if they didn't fully believe something terrible would actually happen to them.

Sneezing has long been linked with beliefs about the well-being of the human soul, and therefore it is no surprise to discover many superstitions relating to this involuntary reflex.

A lot of belief centres on how many times an individual sneezes and what this means. There are many variations of the following rhyme:

One for a kiss,
Two for a wish,
Three for a letter,
Four times something better.
Five for silver,
Six for gold,
Seven for a secret never to be told.

The Ancient Greeks believed that sneezing was a good omen from the gods. In Japan, China and other East Asian countries, sneezing is believed to indicate that you are being talked about. One sneeze and the talk is of good things, two and they are saying bad things about you. A third sneeze and you could well have someone in love with you, but four means impending tragedy.

Dating back to sixteenth-century England, it is often said that sneezing once or three times is an ill omen that should be heeded. Two sneezes, however, were something to wish for, as to sneeze twice augured good luck coming your way. There were exceptions; to sneeze twice for three nights in a row was a sign that there would be a death in the house.

It isn't just human sneezes that are important; if a cat sneezes three times in a row, expect good luck to come your way. In Italian belief, a cat sneezing three times means that everyone in the household runs the risk of catching a cold.

Paying attention to the time of day you sneeze is also good practice. In Iceland, three sneezes before breakfast on a Sunday will bring with it a reward in the week to come. In Kentucky, US, depending on who you talk to, this could mean good luck, or three deaths before the end of the week. Three sneezes are also believed to mean that you will never marry.

SLEEPING WITH A FAN ON AT NIGHT

36

A superstition found predominantly in South Korea, and, to a lesser extent, Japan, is that sleeping with an electric fan on at night in an enclosed room will cause death. The belief has become so widespread over the last few decades that the term "fan death" is now used to describe this strange phenomenon.

To avert tragedy, many in Korea will not use an electric fan unless a window is open at least a fraction. This has extended even further in some cases, with some drivers making sure their vehicle window is open a crack before they turn on their air conditioning. Reports of fan-related deaths proliferated from the 1970s onwards, with a smattering of new cases reported each summer, helping to fuel the already deeply held belief. There is some evidence that this belief is slowly starting to wane among the younger generation.

Many sources state that this curious belief originated in the 1970s, citing a link with the energy crisis of that decade, but there is evidence that fans were regarded with suspicion long before this point. Among others, one article from 1927 states that sitting close to an electric fan can lead to breathing difficulties, headaches and palsy in the facial nerves.

How exactly do fans cause death? Some say that they can cause hypothermia, where a combination of slowed metabolism and cold air from the fan leads to a dangerous plummet in body temperature. Asphyxiation is cited as another cause, as the sleeping person uses up all of the oxygen in the enclosed room and slowly suffocates in their sleep. Some even believe that high levels of carbon dioxide, generated by the fan itself, can lead to death.

So entrenched is this belief that some fan manufacturers issue warnings with their products, stating that hypothermia or suffocation can result from use at night, and The Korean Consumer Protection Board has issued similar warnings. To further reflect the prevalence of this belief, fans in Korea come with a timer setting, to ensure that they are not left on all night.

CUTTING NAILS AT NIGHT

37

According to superstition in Turkey, cutting your nails at night is best avoided, for fear of bringing bad luck to you and your household. This is not an isolated belief, and in the Philippines, cutting finger or toe nails during the night is said to lead to a death in the family. In India, China, Japan, Egypt and Korea, the belief is also shared that cutting nails at night will lead to no good.

Cutting nails at night is a taboo in several countries. In Japan, belief states that you will not be with your parents on their deathbed if you do so. In Malaysia, you are said to be cutting away at your life, and in China you might inadvertently be summoning a ghost. In Egypt, you risk losing belongings or, even worse, causing the death of a loved one.

There is, in fact, a very practical reason not to cut nails at night. In the days before electric lights and nail clippers, attempting to cut your nails in the dark would have been an accident waiting to happen. And while it might not lead to a death, to cut yourself would be bad luck indeed!

Cutting nails on certain days of the week is also seen as a taboo, although there are differing opinions on which days are the least auspicious. Friday and Sunday are generally seen as days to avoid, although this can also vary between and within the same culture. In India, for example, cutting nails on a Tuesday is frowned upon, whereas Wednesday is seen as a good day to do so.

Trying to decide which day is best to cut your nails? Follow this rhyme and you will never go wrong:

> *Cut your nails on Monday, cut them for news;*
> *Cut them on Tuesday, a pair of new shoes;*
> *Cut them on Wednesday, cut them for health;*
> *Cut them on Thursday, cut them for wealth;*
> *Cut them on Friday, cut them for woe;*
> *Cut them on Saturday, a journey you'll go;*
> *Cut them on Sunday, you'll cut them for evil,*
> *For all the next week you'll be ruled by the devil.*

KILLING A SPIDER

38

Many people suffer from the terror of arachnophobia: the fear of spiders. But you might want to think twice the next time you are tempted to squash one; in many places, killing a spider is considered to be extremely unlucky.

A popular saying in both the UK and US is "If you wish to live and thrive, let a spider run alive." There are slight regional variants, but the gist is the same: for a long and prosperous life, leave those spiders roaming free.

Killing a spider is also considered bad luck in Latvia, as it is thought to be a blessing to have one in your home, and therefore to kill the spider is to also kill good fortune with it. Spiders are similarly said to bring good luck in Denmark, and seeing one in the evening is lucky in France.

An eighteenth-century English source relates that it was considered unlucky to kill spiders, but cynically suggests that this was nothing more than an excuse made by slovenly housewives for not dusting away cobwebs more often. There is a saying in Devon: "Who kills a spider, bad luck betides her."

There is particular good luck associated with tiny spiders of the *Linyphiidae* family, more commonly known as money spiders. As the name suggests, seeing one of these, or, even better, having one run across your hand, apparently means good luck in the finance department.

In Sweden and Finland, killing a spider is said to bring rain the following day, and in Qatar, spiders are said to be able to put out fires in the home. In some cultures, the time of day influences whether it is a good or a bad thing to kill a spider. A Japanese saying states, "let spiders live in the morning, kill spiders at night."

Some say that if you cannot avoid killing a spider, bad luck can be avoided by apologizing to it first. However, it might be better not to take the chance, particularly since in Vietnamese belief the soul becomes a spider when you are asleep!

BIRD EXCREMENT

39

Birds, from the smallest sparrow to the most resplendent peacock, are frequently featured in superstitions and folklore. One common belief surrounds a topic best avoided in polite company – what happens if a bird poops on you as it flies by?

Surprising as it may be, it is generally considered good luck if a bird chances to excrete on you. The reason for this is unclear, although most people tend to suggest that the luck comes from how rare an occurrence it is. According to some sources, it is estimated that only around 150,000 people are defecated on by a bird each year. It is said that you have more chance of winning the lottery, and people often buy lottery tickets after such an incident in the hope that their luck will hold!

In England, it has long been considered good luck to have a bird defecate on you, and it is said to herald impending good luck. This particularly held true if it happened on Easter Day. Likewise in Italy, China and Russia, it is seen as a good omen. In Turkey, it is believed that if a bird poops on you, financial good fortune may be on the way.

Some believe that the luck depends on which type of bird has pooped on you. According to some, if you are hit by rook excrement on your way to church in your best clothes, it is a sign that you need to rethink your outfit and return home. The opposite is also held to be true – that it is actually a sign of favour, and you should therefore continue to church safe in the knowledge that your outfit has received approval.

In Australia, there are many jokes and stories surrounding the mythical foo bird. Such tales revolve around the fact that to wipe the excrement from this particular bird away before sunset leads to tragedy and even death, culminating in the punchline: "if the foo shits, wear it."

RAIN ON A WEDDING DAY

40

The flowers are ready, the venue booking has been double-checked, the cake, the wedding attire and guest list are sorted to perfection. Planning a wedding is no mean feat, and reaching the big day with everything in hand is a major achievement indeed. One thing that cannot be predicted or controlled, however, is the weather. Most brides and grooms would be wishing for blue skies and warm sun on their special day, but, according to superstition, they might want to reconsider.

There are relatively few times we would wish for rain during a special event, but it is actually thought in some areas of the world to be good luck if it rains on your wedding day. This is the case in Hindu tradition; it is said that a wet knot is very hard to untie, so if the wedding takes place on a rainy day, then the union between the couple will be particularly long-lasting.

Rain on a wedding day can also be a good sign as it is linked to fertility, suggesting that the couple will have many children in the years ahead. It can also be said to represent a cleansing of all the bad things of the past, leaving the days of marriage ahead to be free of previous sorrow and bad memories. Some say that the rain represents tears, the last that the bride will ever shed in her life!

One of the exceptions to this general rule is in Ireland; there, it is ominously predicted that the bride will cry one tear for every drop of rain that falls on the day. There is also a proverb, "Happy is the bride that the sun shines on," suggesting that newlyweds will fare better if the weather remains bright and dry on their wedding day after all.

TURNING YOUR THUMB AT THE HAGIA SOPHIA

41

One of the world's greatest wonders, Istanbul's Hagia Sophia is a sight to behold, drawing millions of visitors each year. First acting as a Christian Orthodox Church, then a mosque, in the 1930s it was closed for a time before being opened to the public as the museum it is today. Steeped in history and legend, the Hagia Sophia has an enduring and intriguing superstition attached to it.

At the northwest exit of the nave lies a marble pillar that always has a crowd of people around it, waiting to get close. Known variously as the wishing column, sweating column or perspiring column due to the wetness that it exudes, it has a hole in the centre, covered with a metal plate; you should place your thumb in the hole and turn it 360 degrees clockwise; if it comes out wet, then any wish you have made will apparently come true.

Another variation of this practice involves the healing properties the column is said to have. If your thumb or finger emerges wet, then you should rub it on the part of your body that is causing you pain. If you have done it correctly, you will, according to popular belief, be cured of your ailment. This is said to have a long provenance; according to legend, the Byzantine emperor Justinian (527–565 CE) suffered from headaches and leaned his head against the column, only to find his pain gone a short while later!

What causes the wetness that gives the column its name? Some say that it is the tears of the Virgin Mary herself. Other theories suggest that the pillar was touched by St Gregory the miracle worker, and that is how it gained its healing qualities. Scientific explanations cite the porous nature of the column absorbing water from the base as the more mundane cause. Whatever the origin, the column is wet at all times, regardless of the heat of the day, drawing visitors from all over the globe.

GIVING A KNIFE AS A GIFT

Giving gifts is a practice that stretches back into the mists of time; a universally recognized method of conveying friendship, gratitude or respect for the recipient. There are some items that make more problematic gifts than others. When it comes to giving sharp objects such as knives, scissors or even brooches with pins, it is advisable to be aware of one particular superstition.

According to some, if you give or receive a knife as a present, then bad luck awaits you. This can be avoided, however, if you follow one simple step; give the giver a small token payment, so that the knife has been symbolically purchased rather than gifted. Otherwise, the friendship or love between the two parties will be irrevocably severed.

In Croatia, superstition dictates that a small amount is paid after receiving a knife as a gift. This is also true in Russia, where a small monetary token likewise signifies payment. In Latvia, it is believed that money should be given in return when a knife or scissors are given as a gift to reimburse the money spent and to ensure that bad luck doesn't follow.

The belief that knives will sever friendship or love was deeply entrenched in English lore from at least the sixteenth century onwards, and was still going strong in the twentieth century. In Somerset, it was considered very unlucky to be the recipient of a knife or of anything with a pin in it, unless you paid a penny for them. One particular instance records when a brooch was bought for someone as a present and there was an objection made due to the pin, so another gift was chosen instead. Even royalty are not considered immune: the Prince of Wales was presented with a knife during a visit to Sheffield, and gave a Royal Wedding Crown in return, and the Queen herself gave a sixpence when returning scissors used to cut the ribbon at the opening of a new Home Economics Centre, to confirm that no ill was meant by the gesture.

HEARING A COCK CROW

43

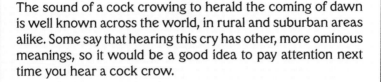

The sound of a cock crowing to herald the coming of dawn is well known across the world, in rural and suburban areas alike. Some say that hearing this cry has other, more ominous meanings, so it would be a good idea to pay attention next time you hear a cock crow.

As early as 65 CE, it was believed that a cock crowing was a bad omen, alerting others to events such as a house fire or a death. The ancients, however, saw it as a victory cry, and so for them it had positive connotations.

In seventeenth-century England, the sound of a cock crow when setting off for a journey reportedly was a bad omen: foretelling of disaster to come. By the mid-twentieth century it was still perceived as a negative experience, and if an expectant mother heard a cock crow on the day she gave birth, it was said that a period of bad luck would follow. In Ireland, apparently if a cock met a person in the doorway and crowed as he or she was setting off for a journey, it was best to think again, as this was a definite sign that everything would go wrong. A cock crowing on your doorstep was generally seen as bad luck, but also well known as a sign that a stranger should be expected.

Throughout history, a cock crowing at a time other than early morning was also often taken as a bad sign. Crowing in the afternoon was a bad omen, and crowing at midnight was seen as particularly ominous, and was said to herald a death. Night-time crowing could also mean that unexpected news was on the way.

According to superstition in the Shetland Isles, Scotland, you should run and feel the feet of a cockerel if it crowed after dark. Warm feet meant good news was on the way, whereas cold feet foretold a death.

If a cockerel clucked like a hen or a hen crowed like a cock, this was also seen as a bad omen.

SPILLING WATER

44

It is generally considered bad luck when we spill something. One exception to this rule, however, is when it comes to spilling water. In some cultures, particularly in Eastern European countries such as Turkey, Serbia and Bulgaria, this intentional act is actually seen to bring good luck.

In Serbia, folklore states that spilling water behind someone will bring them good luck. As a result, people will often throw water behind a loved one on occasions where luck is needed, for instance when they set off on a journey, or when heading to a job interview or an exam. The smooth flowing nature of water is believed to ease the person's way, making things easy for them.

This practice is also popular in Turkey, where a bucket of water is often thrown after a person once farewells have been said. Again, this is due to belief in the fluidity of water; the words *su gibi git, su gibi gel* accompany this ritual, essentially meaning, "go like water, return like water."

Water is said to remove negativity, and, through its flowing nature, take it away from a place or a person. It therefore makes sense that this ritual of spilling water is carried out before important events, and is a common practice by parents when children are starting school. Exams, marriages and graduations are among other times when water is spilled to ensure the future success and happiness of the person or people involved.

In Bulgaria, water is sometimes spilled on the stairs for the intended individual to walk over; be careful before trying this one, as slipping on wet stairs could be far from lucky!

Conversely, in English lore, throwing water out of your house during the night could bring bad luck, as water was said to have protective qualities and would protect the house from evil spirits. Spilling water unintentionally is also generally said to bring bad luck with it.

BEING SEPARATED WHEN WALKING

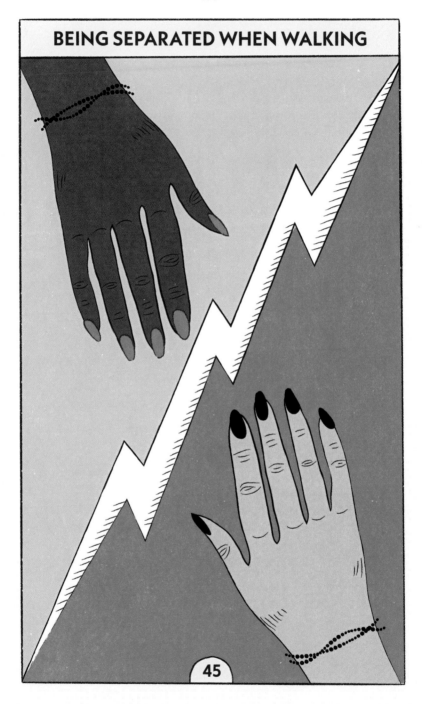

45

A common occurrence when walking down the road with a friend is that an obstacle, such as a pillar or a post, comes into view. No problem, you separate, one passing on each side of the obstruction before coming back together again. According to a widespread superstition, however, this might not be such a good idea.

The general belief states that to split up around an obstacle is to bring bad luck and to sever the connection between the two people, either breaking their relationship through a quarrel, or, literally, keeping them physically apart. Some refer to this separation as "splitting the pole". In a similar vein, in Albania, separating two people who are talking together is said to lead to an argument. The crisis can apparently be averted though if those involved utter the words "bread and butter".

There is some differing in opinion regarding whether both parties have to say the words, or if just one person uttering the phrase is enough to avoid the bad luck. Some say that the superstition only applies if the two people had linked arms or hands and had to unlink in order to walk around the obstacle.

The origins of this particular superstition are unknown, but there are several suggestions. Some say that it is because bread and butter are such a well-known pairing, representing the close connection between the two people who do not want their relationship broken. Others believe it is because once a piece of bread is buttered, it cannot be undone, much like the bond between those separated temporarily by the obstacle.

People also have different ideas about how to undo the bad luck attracted by splitting up. Suggestions include spinning three times or saying "salt and pepper".

Of course, you could always err on the side of caution and make sure that both people pass on the same side when walking around something!

DROPPING A GLOVE

46

Gloves, in different forms and materials, have been a staple of life for centuries, variously offering protection and warmth or acting as a fashion statement. Coming in a pair, gloves are particularly prone to being dropped, and according to superstition, this might have unforeseen consequences.

A general belief states that if you drop a glove, someone else should be the one to pick it up again. If you pick the glove up yourself, you are likely to experience a disappointment or bad luck in the near future. When someone else picks the glove up, some say that you will receive a – hopefully pleasant – surprise instead. Some say that this is linked to the old belief that only a lover should pick up a lady's glove, or to times when a glove was dropped in the hope that a love interest would pick it up.

If someone does do you the favour of picking up a glove for you, you aren't out of the woods yet. Although the natural thing to do is to thank them for their efforts, some believe that to say "thank you" will lead to dire consequences.

Gloves are said to have been used in the past as a form of secret communication between would-be lovers, desperate to pass signals between each other without being detected by sharp-eyed observers. Dropping both gloves was said to mean "I love you", while dropping one provided a resounding "yes". Woe betide the poor person whose companion turned their gloves inside out, since this message meant "I hate you".

It is also said to be bad luck to give gloves as a gift. If you do, make sure to ask for a token in return in "payment", otherwise it is thought that both you and the receiver will be in danger of attracting bad luck or of arguing with a friend.

A BLACK CAT CROSSING YOUR PATH

47

Black cats have received a lot of bad press over the years, and are often erroneously associated with witches, darkness and evil magic. One common superstition involves the belief that bad luck will come if a black cat crosses your path. But just how unlucky is a black cat?

A black cat crossing your path is a sign of bad luck in Turkey; this can be counteracted by quickly touching something black. In the town of La Harpe, Illinois, US, it was believed that it was bad luck for a black cat to cross your path. If it came to your house, however, then that was another matter, and good luck would follow. In the Netherlands and Denmark, a black cat crossing your path is also seen as bad luck, a belief held across many areas of Europe. In Norway and Sweden, if one crosses your path you should spit three times to avoid bad luck. For some, it depends on which direction the cat is passing; in Germany, if a cat passes left to right then you can relax, good times are coming. If it's right to left, however, it is thought that bad luck is on the way. In China, black cats are linked to poverty and hunger.

It is not black cats but rather white ones that have been associated with bad luck in the UK; black cats have traditionally been seen as lucky. In Wales, and some areas of England, the bad luck of a white cat could be cancelled out only if you also had a pure black cat to go with it. If a black cat turned up on your doorstep, you would be wise to invite it in, as it was said to bring good luck. If the cat was lost, then bad luck would swiftly follow. In Yorkshire, black cats were said to protect fishermen at sea if one was kept indoors. In Japan, a black cat crossing your path is also seen as a good sign, while in India, seeing three black cats together is believed to be a good omen indeed.

SPEAKING AT THE SAME TIME

48

Have you ever had that moment where you say the exact same thing as the person you are with? Although this might be taken as a sign that you are completely in tune with your companion, speaking at the same time has been said to have several other meanings around the world.

An eighteenth-century English belief stated that if someone said something another person was about to say, the first speaker would be the first to marry. Likewise, the person to finish speaking first would also marry first.

Another result of speaking at the same time relates to making wishes. In England in the late nineteenth century, it was said that when two people said the same thing at the same time they should hook their little fingers together and make a wish – the wish would then come true. This belief extended into the twentieth century, and the ritual seems to have grown in complexity over time. In Somerset, the two were not to say any other words but should hook the fingers of their right hands together, name a poet out loud, and make a wish in silence. Neither Shakespeare or Burns should be mentioned, however, or the wish would not come true. A further small verse could be added afterwards to ensure the outcome of the wish.

In Suffolk, the pair should touch wood, touch their knee and then whistle. The first person to complete the actions would then apparently receive a letter. American belief suggests linking little fingers, making a wish, and saying "thumbs." A poet is then named, before a complex series of questions and utterances occur to ensure the wishes come true.

In Estonia, if two people say the same thing at the same time, bad luck is also apparently counteracted by a somewhat complex ritual. The pair must make a wish, hook little fingers together, count to three and then say "Adam" or "Eve." The wish is then said to come true: but only if both say the same name!

Today, when two people say the same phrase or word, each rushes to say "jinx" first. The person who says it last loses.

A STOPPED CLOCK

49

A clock stopping is not an uncommon occurrence. Whether it's due to a battery running out or in the case of an ornate grandfather clock, the mechanism running down, a stopped clock is little more than an easily rectified inconvenience. However, sometimes a clock stops without any known reason, and this is another matter altogether.

Time and life – or the ending of it – have often been linked. In the nineteenth century, clocks were purposefully stopped to mark the time of death when someone passed, so the stopped clock is a symbol of the ending of life. A spontaneously stopping clock was seen as an ominous sign, and it was often said that the time shown on the clock at the point where it stopped was the time that a death would occur. Supporting this, there are many anecdotal tales of clocks stopping at the exact time of death of a celebrity or member of royalty. There are also accounts of clocks stopping just before a death was to occur.

A clock striking at the wrong time, or chiming a non-existent time – 13 chimes is common – is also said to be a sign of a death to come. In Wales, it was believed that if two clocks struck at the exact same moment, tragedy would follow, as a married couple in the local area would die. American Reverend Samuel Watson recorded a stopped clock striking before the death of his wife and two of his children, in his book of 1873.

According to popular belief, it is also wise to be careful where in the room you position your clock. If it is facing the fire, it is thought that the fire will go out.

In China, it is considered bad luck to give a clock as a gift. It is believed to herald a death or a funeral, as the word for "clock" and "end" sound the same. Watches, however, are frequently given as gifts and are exempt from this taboo since this similarity doesn't apply to the word "watch".

CALLING A BABY CUTE

50

Babies are generally considered cute and adorable, and even those who aren't baby people will want to do the polite thing where new parents are concerned. The temptation might be strong to tell the proud new parents that their offspring is the sweetest thing you've ever seen, but according to one particular superstition that is not actually a good idea.

In Vietnam, it is said that calling a baby cute will mean that they grow up with a less than attractive appearance. It might feel strange, but if you want to convey that you find a baby lovely, telling them in a suitably cooing tone that they are ugly will be much more appreciated than sharing your true opinion. In Thailand and elsewhere in South-East Asia, it is said that good-looking babies are in danger of being stolen by ghosts or evil spirits. Babies are called "ugly cute" and sometimes a smudge of kohl is put on their faces to make them appear less attractive.

Bulgarian practice also counsels against praising a baby's appearance; to do so will apparently make the Devil jealous. To avoid this, pretend to spit on the baby; wishing them negative experiences as you do so should also help to avoid arousing the Devil's envy.

Belief in Serbia holds that calling a baby cute or similar will condemn them to a life filled with bad luck, whereas calling them ugly ensures the opposite. In Egypt, it is also considered bad luck to call a baby cute, and people are advised to call them ugly instead, to keep the bad fortune away. In China, it is similarly agreed that praising a baby is a bad idea, as it could attract evil spirits.

In some countries, such as India, Romania and Greece, if a baby is paid a compliment someone will spit near or even on the baby, in order to ward off the evil eye. In Turkey, the evil eye is likewise feared, and cute children are called ugly to avoid arousing any jealousy.

LETTING A BABY LOOK IN A MIRROR

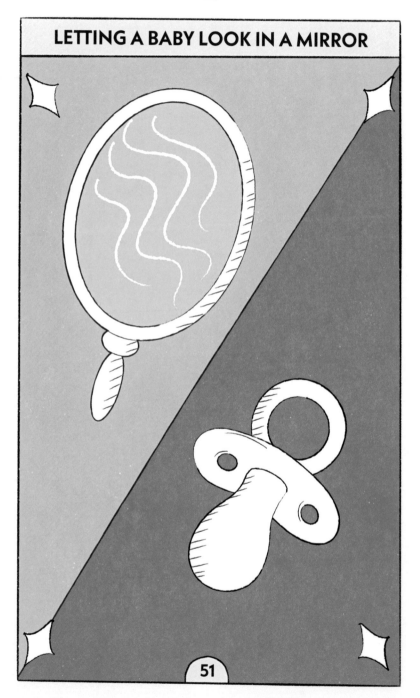

Many modern baby toys and books come complete with mirrors, with the idea that not only will the infant be entertained, but will also start to grow acquainted with their own features. According to superstition, however, this could be risky business indeed before the child is a year old, and might put them in danger of all manner of horrifying consequences.

In India, it is thought that if a baby looks in a mirror before they are a year old, then they run the risk of being reminded of their previous life. It is said that they might also end up with crooked teeth. In some areas of Africa, it was likewise thought that a child might be in danger of remembering their past life, or of having their soul stolen. In areas of Asia such as Singapore, it is believed that the child's soul will be stolen away if they look in a mirror before they are one, referencing a common belief that the soul could become trapped in a mirror. In Greece, if a baby sees their own reflection in a mirror before they have been baptized, it is said that their soul will be stolen away.

In England, it was widely believed that letting a baby look in a mirror was not a good idea, a belief that dated from at least the nineteenth century. In Northamptonshire, it was believed that it would do a baby great harm. In Suffolk, it was said that a baby who saw themselves in a mirror would go cross eyed, and according to belief in early twentieth-century Somerset, their lives would be plagued by trouble. Other potential fates included developing a stutter, becoming a thief, growing up vain, developing rickets or dying before the year was out.

There was some difference in opinion in when the danger period was over; sometimes looking in a mirror was considered safe after four or six months old, but the most common age advised to wait until was one year old.

TAKING BANANAS ON A BOAT

A favourite fruit with many, bananas are more often seen as a sign of fun – for instance, when someone slips on a discarded banana skin in a cartoon – than a symbol of menace. There is one area, however, where bananas are no laughing matter. According to a superstition held across much of the world, from Australia to Turkey to the US, it is seen as bad luck to take bananas on a boat.

It is unclear exactly where this prevalent belief originated, but one thing is certain – it holds a great deal of sway today for those with fishing or shipping connections. One suggested origin is that it stems from the days of dangerous sea voyages; when a ship went down, bananas were one of the few things that would float, and they therefore became associated with shipwrecks. Another theory is that they were seen as bad luck due to the spiders, insects and other creatures that might stow away in the bunches. Others suggest that having perishable cargo on board meant that there was no time for fishing, and as a result the fruit has become linked over time with a poor catch and therefore bad luck.

This belief is held strongly today by those who fish for sport. The presence of bananas on board is blamed for a lack of fish, but also for other, more ominous, happenings, such as engine failure and mechanical mishaps.

The belief is so entrenched that there are many in the charter fishing business who ban anything associated with bananas completely from being on board. This doesn't just include foods containing the fruit, but also anything with a banana pictured on it, including logos, or even anything that could be construed as banana shaped.

In the town of Portsoy, Aberdeenshire, bananas were banned before their annual boat festival in 2015 as a nod to this superstition. Even banana-flavoured ice cream was removed from the local ice cream shop until the event was over!

WRITING IN RED INK

According to Chinese, Korean and Japanese belief, writing names in red ink is best avoided. The colour red is believed to be closely linked with death – readily bringing to mind blood, pain and dying – and for this reason, writing in red pen is considered unlucky. To write your own name – or that of another living person – in red ink, is seen as an omen of death.

In China, the names of convicted criminals were once written in red – first in chicken's blood, then eventually red ink. As a result, it is a bad idea to write the name of a living person in red ink, as it is linking them to death and perhaps summoning death to them. Names on gravestones were also written in red, continuing the connection between red ink and death. Despite this, the colour red in itself is not unlucky in China and Chinese communities; quite the opposite, as red is a symbol of good luck when worn at weddings and is used liberally in decorations during Chinese New Year.

Japanese belief also associates red ink with death due to names being written in that colour on tombs while a person still lives; upon death, the red ink is replaced with black. Writing a name in red ink can also cause offence as it can suggest a person was a criminal since the names of criminals were once written in red. Red ink can also suggest a person will soon face bankruptcy and financial ruin.

In Korea, writing the name of a living person in red ink is frowned upon because red ink was used to record the name of a deceased person on the family register. The red is believed to ward off evil spirits, but if the person still lives then the opposite might occur. To write a name in red when the person was still alive was to wish harm or even death for them. There is one exception: red ink is used for name stamps in place of signatures, and this is not considered harmful.

TETRAPHOBIA – FEAR OF THE NUMBER FOUR

54

4

A number that is considered to be hugely unlucky in some areas of the world is the number four. This belief is most commonly held in the nations of East Asia, or areas with large Chinese communities, and tetraphobia – fear of the number four – runs even deeper than fear of the number 13.

Why is the number four so feared? In many forms of Chinese, the word "four" sounds very similar to that of "death". In Japanese and Korean, the words sound identical. The link between the number four and bad luck is therefore obvious, with people going out of their way to avoid any link with the number.

This fear translates into an avoidance of the number four in everything from building floors and hotel rooms to car registration plates. In some cases, any number with a four in it is avoided. In Mandarin, 14 and 74 are also avoided, as they sound like "is dead" or "will be dead" and "is already dead", while in Cantonese, 14 and 24 are even more taboo, meaning "must die" and "easy to die" respectively. Some apartment blocks skip all floors from 40–49. In Singapore, some public transport companies don't use the number four in their registration plates and serial numbers, while South Korean numbering systems in hospitals and other public buildings also omit four. In Japan, 49 is also unlucky as it sounds like "pain until death".

Those who consider the number four unlucky not only avoid the number itself, but avoid doing or giving things in fours or multiples of four, and the number is not spoken or referenced unless absolutely necessary. People often avoid important things such as appointments or celebrations on the fourth of a month, or even on a date with a four in it.

An intriguing study investigating US mortality figures revealed that on the fourth day of a month, people of Chinese or Japanese heritage with a pre-existing heart condition were 13 per cent more likely to die of a heart attack than on any other day of the month, suggesting a potential link between cultural beliefs and an actual physical manifestation of this huge psychological stress.

SLEEPING WITH YOUR HEAD FACING NORTH

55

Have you ever wondered whether the direction you sleep in is relevant to whether you get a good night's sleep or not, or even if it will impact your life in other ways? According to superstition across the world, it might be a good idea to take note of where your head lies next time you settle down for the night.

The most common belief regarding sleeping direction is that it is best to sleep with your head facing towards the north. In nineteenth-century Ireland, a person who was unwell was advised to sleep facing north to south, and not, under any circumstances, east to west. In England, it was generally believed that a better night's sleep would be had with the head facing to the north, something that persisted through the twentieth century and onwards. Sleeping from east to west was said to be far inferior. A seventeenth-century belief stated that if a person's bed was set to the north, then they would have male children. Sleeping with your head to the north is also believed by some to bring wealth and money.

The reason for this belief does have its basis in science, although there is no actual evidence to support this particular superstition. The idea has its roots in the knowledge of the magnetic north. It is believed that the magnetic waves between the two poles of north and south would help soothe a person to sleep. In contrast, sleeping facing east to west would lead to disturbances, as it went across the magnetic pull. Although this has been disproven, the belief persists.

In Japan, however, sleeping with your head to the north is advised against, as this was the direction that corpses were laid out. According to the Chinese art of Feng Shui, sleeping north to south is also generally a bad idea. In India, sleeping to the east or south is thought to be best, and in Madagascar, sleeping with your head to the north was seen as a sign of being a witch!

POINTING

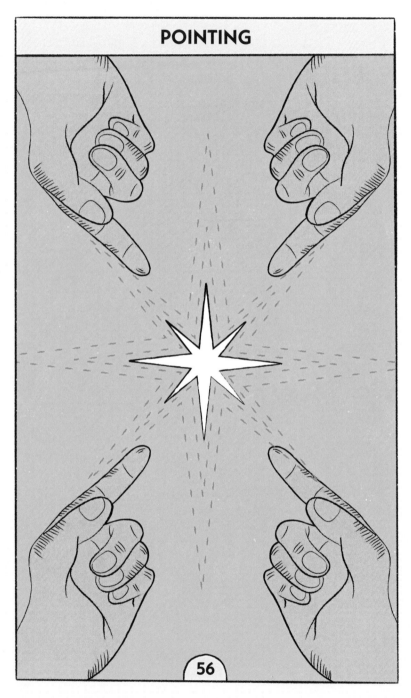

56

Pointing is a useful gesture for indicating a person or a direction, or for generally getting a point across. It is one of those milestones that we wait for in babies, but, by the time we reach a more advanced age, it is often considered to be rude. What if there were more to it than just manners or lack of them? In many cultures and countries, pointing at specific objects is thought to bring with it a great deal of bad luck.

Chinese belief holds that to point at the moon is a very bad idea indeed; doing so will lead to your ears getting cut off by a vengeful spirit. However, this might just be a way to discourage children from pointing at it, as it is considered disrespectful. In Singapore and Malaysia, it is also seen as bad luck to point at the moon, which apparently will result in the back of your ears being cut.

Pointing at celestial objects is generally frowned upon, as it is thought to anger the gods. Pointing at the moon, the sun and the stars is therefore considered taboo in a number of cultures. It is considered disrespectful. In Thailand, pointing at rainbows should be avoided: it is said one of your fingers will fall off.

In England, pointing towards faeces is considered to be bad luck and should be avoided. In Germany, pointing is not only considered disrespectful, it is also thought to bring bad luck.

The forefinger or index finger, most often used for pointing, has long been considered bad and vulgar in English belief right up until at least the twentieth century and it was even considered poisonous. According to traditional belief, this finger shouldn't be used to apply any sort of salve or ointment due to the risk of poisoning or infection.

In the US, beware of pointing at a shooting star. To do so is thought to lead to a death in the family.

Pointing at a grave is frowned upon in Turkey, as it is believed that this will destroy the vitality of an individual, leading to them growing thin and weak.

SAYING "HAPPY BIRTHDAY" EARLY

57

Celebrating birthdays, especially significant ones, can be a lot of fun – presents, friends, cake, good food and good company – what isn't to like? It is tempting therefore to spread the fun out over a series of days, but superstition says that might actually not be the best idea if you want to keep your luck for the year ahead.

In many areas, it is considered extremely taboo to wish someone a happy birthday or to celebrate a birthday before the exact date; even doing so a few hours early is deeply frowned upon. The reason for this is that it is said to bring bad luck, and who wants bad luck on their birthday?

Argentinian Pope Francis referenced this belief in 2018, expressing the fact that to wish someone a happy birthday ahead of the important day was said to bring bad luck. The person wishing you the happy birthday early is effectively jinxing your life, which is a poor birthday gift indeed!

In Russia, it is also said to be bad manners to wish someone happy birthday early or to have any form of celebration; bad luck will surely come to whoever tries it, so it is best avoided. This is also believed in Spain; *feliz dia*, happy day, should be wished instead on the days approaching the big day itself.

Belief in India similarly follows this trend. Celebrating a birthday early is seen as arrogance in the assumption that the person in question will make it to their next birthday: something no one can ever guarantee. Therefore, celebrating, giving presents or even saying "happy birthday" early will bring bad luck, implying a great confidence – perhaps unfounded – in the length of a person's life.

And so, although the urge to celebrate early can be strong, according to superstition it might be best to wait!

SLEEPING IN THE MOONLIGHT

58

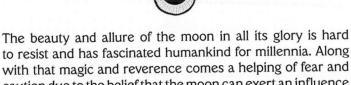

The beauty and allure of the moon in all its glory is hard to resist and has fascinated humankind for millennia. Along with that magic and reverence comes a helping of fear and caution due to the belief that the moon can exert an influence on our fragile human forms. One particular superstition relates to this – the belief that sleeping in moonlight should be avoided.

The idea that moonlight could adversely affect the human brain, particularly when a person was sleeping unawares, has a long provenance. Sleeping in moonlight has been considered risky business indeed: it could apparently leave you insane, blind, or even, according to some, in danger of becoming a werewolf!

According to an old Irish superstition, if the moon shines on the face of someone while they sleep, they will find themselves "moonstruck" and reduced to a state of insanity. It was also thought to lead to a form of blindness. This belief continued well into the twentieth century and beyond; children were still being told not to sleep with moonlight on their faces in England and Ireland at that time. Nineteenth-century sailors were also cautioned against sleeping on the upper deck when the moon was full.

Moonlight has been linked to bad luck in general, and some say that it is bad luck to be born in the moonlight. In Turkey, however, it is considered lucky if you are born when there is a full moon, and you are thought to have a bright future ahead of you. Drinking water that has had the moon shine on it, however, is another matter, and whoever drinks it is said to have bad luck. English mothers even went so far as not to hang out their baby's nappies in the moonlight, due to the belief that bad luck would follow. In Austria, be careful not to look at the new moon for too long; this will apparently make you sneeze and bad luck will follow.

If you do happen to wake and find the moon shining down on you, it might be advisable to pull the curtains – just in case!

WALKING BACKWARDS

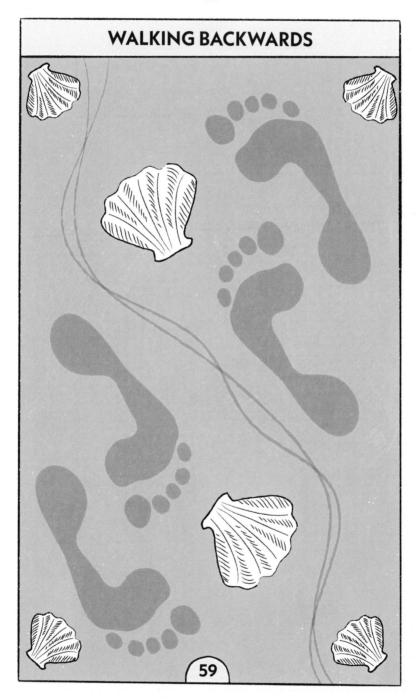

When walking, it makes sense to face the direction in which you wish to go. After all, who wants to run the risk of walking into something or someone? But practicalities aside, walking backwards is also considered to be bad luck according to superstition in various areas of the world.

In nineteenth-century England, children were frequently cautioned against walking backwards when setting off. If they didn't heed this advice, according to superstition they ran the risk of general bad luck, having an unsuccessful outcome to their errand, or even that their mother might die.

In Portugal, walking backwards has links with the Devil; according to superstition, the Devil himself walks that way, and who would want to walk the same way as the Devil? Italian belief also cautions against walking backwards because of the Devil; because it shows him where you are going, and he can therefore follow you and cause havoc in your life. Some also say that walking backwards will mean you see a witch when midnight arrives.

Have you ever dreamed of walking backwards? According to some, this can mean that either obstacles are in your path or that you have lost your way in life. It might be time to make some changes!

There are exceptions to every rule, however, and there are some instances when walking backwards is considered a good thing. If you've attracted bad luck by walking under a ladder, just make sure you walk out backwards and the bad luck will be averted. Walking backwards is also sometimes said to protect against evil spirits; walking backwards into the house will mean that the spirits can't follow you inside. Have you ever accidentally carried a hoe into the house and brought about bad luck? No problem, just make sure you carry it out again while walking backwards through the same door you entered by, and the bad luck will be reversed.

EATING THE LAST PIECE OF FOOD

60

There is a whole wealth of etiquette surrounding food, and customs and traditions vary from time to time and place to place the world over. At occasions such as a party, wedding or family meal, shared food on communal plates is common, but what happens when there is only one piece of food left – should you take it or not?

Belief differs on this matter from country to country, but the overall feeling is that the last piece of something is important. It is so important, in fact, that several countries even have a name for it. In Bulgaria, if someone offers you the last piece then you won't be any the worse for taking it, but *only* if you are offered it. If you just take it, then you are eating what is known as the shame piece. In Germany, that last slice of cake or other food that everyone secretly wants, is known as the *anstandsstuck* or decency piece; if it is left uneaten, then good luck will follow. In Spain, it is known as *la de la vergüenza* – the one of shame. It is considered the height of bad manners to take the last remaining piece, and it will often remain on the plate right until the end of the event or meal.

In some Asian countries, eating the last piece of food on a shared plate is said to lead to life as a spinster. Likewise in some areas of the US, it is said that you will become an old maid if you eat or drink the last bit. Irish belief dictates that you will have a solitary life; not necessarily a bad thing! In Thailand, on the other hand, if you eat the last piece, you will end up with an attractive partner.

Conversely, in some countries it is considered bad luck to leave food on your plate, and children are often told this to encourage them to not waste food. In Germany, it apparently means the sun won't shine. In the Philippines, the number of pieces of rice left on your plate supposedly determines how many days you spend in purgatory!

SITTING AT THE CORNER OF THE TABLE

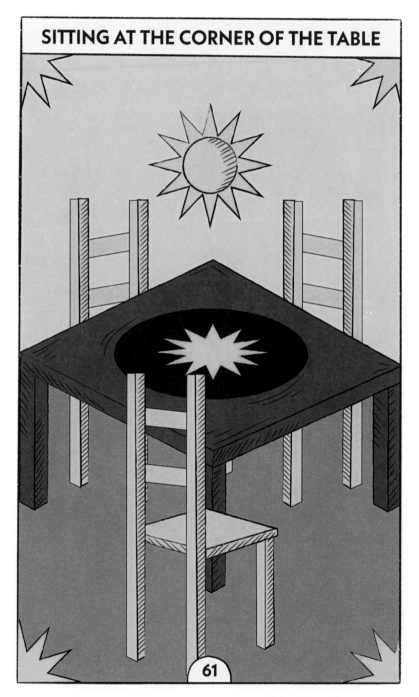

61

Have you ever paid much attention to your position when you sit down at the table to eat? According to this superstition you should, as sitting at the corner of the table brings with it a fate that many would wish to avoid.

A popular superstition in Russia, it is said that if someone sits at the corner of the table, they run the risk of attracting bad luck. It is believed that the person in question will not marry; either for seven years, or never at all. Due to this, it is ill-advised for young unmarried women in particular to sit at the corner of the table, and they will likely be directed to sit elsewhere. Married women, and children who can wait out the seven years, are fine to sit where they like!

This superstition is also held in Hungary, where sitting at the corner of the table is similarly associated with the bad luck of not finding a partner. In Lithuania, the single person can expect to remain in that state for seven years if they find themselves with a corner seat, whereas in Poland, it is said that they will remain single forever. It is up to the individual to decide whether this counts as bad luck or good! In the Ukraine, it is also said that those who sit at the corner of the table will not marry.

Where does this superstition come from? One suggested origin is that the corner of the table was traditionally the position where old maids were seated during gatherings, and, since being unmarried was often viewed as a bad thing by others, over time, this position came to stand for bad luck in itself.

LEAVING EMPTY BOTTLES ON THE FLOOR

62

When out with friends or family, many like to have a drink or two, particularly if celebrating a special occasion. When you finish a bottle, however, be sure to remove it from the table and place it on the floor, otherwise bad luck could be coming your way.

This superstition seems to be specific to Russia, where it is believed that it is bad luck to leave empty bottles on the bar or on your table at a restaurant. Some go even further and say that empty bottles should even be removed from the table at home and placed on the floor instead, just in case. This is such an entrenched belief that it is said that waiting staff will quickly remove a bottle if you are not quick enough to place it on the floor. Failing to do so is said to mean either suffering in your future, or less prosperous times ahead.

It is thought that this curious superstition derives from when Cossack soldiers were in France in the first half of the nineteenth century. They realized that the Parisian restaurant owners had a novel way of charging customers. Instead of taking payment per bottle ordered, it is said that they charged for each bottle that was left on the table. The savvy soldiers quickly worked out that hiding their empty bottles under the table therefore meant a greatly reduced bill. When they returned to Russia, so the legend goes, they brought the practice back with them, and the superstition remains today.

Another potential origin is that empty containers might provide a hiding place for evil spirits. Leaving your empty bottles on the table therefore could be an invitation for such a spirit to take up residence, while hiding them on the floor makes that eventuality more unlikely.

EXAM LUCK

63

Exams are a nerve-wracking experience for many the world over, with the days leading up to the big event filled with revision, worry and prayers that all will go well. Because of this, there are countless superstitions that have built up around exam time, with the hope that following them will lead to a successful outcome.

One such superstition from South Korea is the idea that hair shouldn't be washed before an exam, for fear of washing all the hard-earned knowledge out of your head at the vital moment. This is also believed in the Philippines, and in Russia, where shaving should also be avoided. In India, taking a bath before an exam is a no-no for similar reasons.

What you wear to an exam is also said to influence the result. In the Philippines and China, wearing something red, often underwear, is advised. Although be aware that red is also the colour used to write scores that are fails, so you might want to think twice.

Eating particular foods beforehand is a common exam superstition. In Vietnam, it is believed that eggs should be avoided before exams since they look like a zero and that might be the grade you get. In Singapore, Hong Kong and Malaysia, chicken juice is thought to boost brain power, and is often drunk in the lead up to exam time. The Chinese word for kiwi sounds the same as "easy to pass exams", so for obvious reasons kiwis are often eaten to encourage success. In Japan, katsudon is eaten prior to an exam, because it is close to "katsu" which means winning and is therefore thought to bring good luck.

In Poland, students entering the exam room should be kicked in order to ensure they get a good grade.

Finally, remember to kick your chair when it is all over and you are on your way out of the exam room – this is to ensure that you never have to return there again to re-sit the exam!

SINGING AT THE DINNER TABLE

64

Singing is a popular past-time, and some people just can't hold back when the urge to belt out a tune takes hold. According to some, however, it might be a good idea to restrain yourself if you feel like having a warble when at the dinner table, as singing at the table is said to bring bad luck with it.

In Somerset in the early twentieth century, it was believed that to sing during a meal would lead to disappointment of some kind. Mid-century Scottish belief, however, warned that singing at dinner would lead to death in the poor house for the singer.

It is likely that this taboo about singing at the table is linked to ideas of etiquette and manners and that it was bad manners to sing while sitting down to eat. Some say that singing during a meal means your future partner will be insane. In the Netherlands, singing at the dining table is said to bring severe consequences. It is thought that you are singing to the Devil for your dinner and bringing yourself bad luck with it.

It is not only at the table that you should be careful – singing while cooking is also fraught with danger. Some say that doing so will mean you end up being a widow or never marrying. A Malaysian superstition states that you will end up marrying someone who is very boring.

Singing before breakfast in general is frowned upon in English and Scottish superstition, signifying that someone who is happy before breakfast will find themselves with upset later in the day. Some believe that singing should be avoided before this first, important meal of the day. In Cornwall, it was said that: "if you sing afore bite, you will cry before night." While a Russian belief says that it will bring bad luck for the remainder of the year.

TREADING IN DOG EXCREMENT

65

It's a sorry fact of life that from time to time you will likely have trodden in dog poop. It's a nuisance, not to mention a health hazard, and there is just no way to put a good spin on it – muck on your shoe is a bad deal. Or so you would think! According to some, treading in dog excrement can have hidden merits after all.

In France, it is a popular superstition that treading in dog muck is good luck. This is only if you step in it with your left foot, however; if you happen to step in the mess with your right foot, then your luck remains as bad as you would expect. Paris, in particular, has long been famous for having large quantities of dog poop, so it shouldn't be too hard to put this superstition to the test there!

In England, the idea that treading in excrement means good luck dates back to at least the seventeenth century, with phrases such as "muck is luck" suggesting that getting poop on your foot was not always the disaster it might appear. This belief was still prevalent in the late nineteenth century, with the phrase "shitten luck is good luck". If you did happen to tread in muck when on the way to a wedding, it was considered bad luck to wipe it off again, and the unfortunate person should therefore keep it on their foot as they continued on their way. Towards the end of the twentieth century, "where there's muck, there's luck" was said in Essex, showing that the idea still held traction in the minds of many people.

This didn't just hold true for dog excrement; it was also considered lucky to tread in horse manure or a cow pat!

A FLY IN YOUR DRINK

66

At the end of a long, hard day, you sit down to put your feet up, looking forward to a much-deserved cup of tea. Or perhaps you are out with friends and about to enjoy a glass of wine or a beer. Imagine then looking down and finding a fly floating around in your drink! You would be forgiven for thinking that your luck was very bad indeed, but according to superstition that isn't always the case.

According to nineteenth-century fishermen of Greenock, Renfrewshire, Scotland, having a fly fall into the drink you were about to drink or were in the process of drinking was something to be very pleased about, as it was a certain omen of good luck to come. In twentieth-century Somerset, England, a fly in your cup of tea, while an irritation, was also a sign of good luck.

Some say that if a fly ends up in your cup or glass, it is best to submerge the fly entirely in the drink. This is due to a belief that one wing holds a disease, while the other the antidote, and as it is impossible to tell which is which, the whole fly needs to go under just to make sure.

If a fly flies across your face three times before landing on it, beware, since this might mean you are going to fall sick and perhaps die. If this happens on your hand, it is a good sign, and money is said to be coming your way.

In England, until at least the twentieth century, the last fly of the year was said to be lucky, and most certainly shouldn't be killed. Therefore, if you see a fly in the last few days or weeks before the New Year, it is best to leave it be to avoid bad luck.

Although lucky in a drink, if a fly ends up in the ink of an inkstand it is said to be a sign of bad luck.

THUNDER – GOOD OR BAD LUCK?

67

Thunder has long been credited with having the power to predict events to come; as far back as Roman author Pliny the Elder writing in 77 CE, it was believed that thunder claps could be used to ascertain what was to happen on a day in the future, or even to reveal matters that had been kept concealed. The belief that thunder occurring to the left is lucky also stems from this time.

According to a popular rhyme from the sixteenth century, the day of the week on which thunder occurred influenced what would happen. Thunder on a Sunday meant the death of a learned man, whereas thunder on a Monday signalled the death of a woman. Tuesdays would merely mean rain, whereas a harlot would perish if it thundered on a Wednesday. Thunder on a Thursday would mean an abundance of corn and sheep; on a Friday the murder of a great man; and thunder on a Saturday would bring plague and death.

Thunder was often seen as a sign of displeasure of the gods; in Norse mythology it was a sign of Thor's anger, and in twentieth-century England it was said to be God reminding humankind of their many faults. Thursdays were thought to be an unlucky day to set sail, due to it being Thor's day and therefore linked to thunder and storms.

Thunder was, however, also seen as a good sign; its occurrence after the coronation of Charles II of England in 1661 was taken as a good omen by many people. Thunder in a clear sky is generally seen as good luck, as is an uneven number of thunder claps in quick succession. Thunder is also useful as it is said to predict the weather for the months to come; for example, thunder in February is thought to mean that snow will come in May.

It was believed that a tree struck by lightning had the power to cure toothache; according to Pliny the Elder, biting off a piece of wood and applying it to the tooth would cure the pain. This was still believed in the late nineteenth century, when chewing bark from a tree that had been struck by lightning was likewise believed to cure toothache.

WALKING OVER DRAINS

68

Manhole covers are a familiar sight when walking along pavements, and many people don't give them a second thought. According to Swedish superstition, however, it is best to be watching where you step, for walking over them has the potential to bring all manner of disaster.

In Sweden, manhole covers have one of two letters on them: K or A. K stands for *kallvatten*, Swedish for fresh or cold water, while A is for *avlopp*, or sewage, but according to superstition, these two letters have another meaning. K also represents *kärlek*, the Swedish word for love, with A standing for *avbruten*, meaning interrupted, and therefore heartbreak or broken love. It stands to reason then that people often avoid walking on drain covers marked with A, while going out of their way to tread on those marked with K. For even better luck in love, it is said that you should stand on the cover for a moment and think of the person you love, or, if you can manage it, kissing on the K cover is even luckier.

If you accidentally step on the wrong cover, all is not lost. If someone – unsolicited – comes and pats you on the back three times, then the bad luck can be averted. Make sure not to ask someone for help though, as it won't count! For general good luck, jumping on the K cover – the more times the better – is advised.

In England, there is also a superstition regarding drain covers, focusing on how many covers you walk over. Some say that two drain covers together is good luck, but walking over three is bad luck. This can be overridden by finding a single drain cover and walking over that, or the less sanitary practice of spitting on the ground or on the middle cover. Some say that walking over three covers is bad luck because together they are the same length as a coffin.

GIVING YELLOW FLOWERS

69

Flowers can brighten up any room, and giving them as a gift to those we like and love has been a popular choice throughout the ages. Yellow blooms are particularly cheerful, and due to their brightness and ability to conjure up warmth and joy, it is easy to see why they might be high on the list of favourites. Giving yellow flowers, however, is not as straight forward as you might think, and some say that they are a bad choice of offering.

In Russia, in particular, giving yellow flowers to a loved one is a definite no-no. Yellow is considered to be the colour of unfaithfulness, and giving someone a bouquet of yellow flowers is dooming them to infidelity in the near future. Yellow flowers are also thought to lead to arguments and the inevitable end of a relationship, which is probably not your intent when giving someone flowers! There is even a song, 'Yellow Tulips', which is a well-known breakup song. Yellow flowers are also frowned upon as a gift in the Ukraine. Yellow flowers have historically been used as a rebuff; in the late nineteenth century, they were used to tell a potential love interest that their affections were sadly not returned.

Ancient Egyptian and Mayan cultures, however, viewed yellow flowers favourably. Mayans saw them as a sign of great abundance, and Egyptians thought them valuable due to sharing a colour with gold and the sun itself.

In the UK and US, yellow flowers today are a symbol of friendship, yellow roses in particular. In Paris and Lyon in France, yellow flowers stand for jealousy. In Central and Southern America, yellow flowers are strongly associated with death; they are used to decorate the graves of the dead, and in particular in Mexico on *Dia de los Muertos*, the Day of the Dead, yellow marigolds are placed on graves of dead relatives.

BURNING CHRISTMAS EVERGREENS

70

However you celebrate, nothing says Christmas or the mid-winter festivities like some decorative evergreens. Attractive to look at, and imbued with great significance and meaning, evergreens such as holly and ivy have been associated with mid-winter since pre-Christian times. According to superstition, however, you should be very careful how you dispose of your decorative greenery once the festivities are over, otherwise you could be courting disaster.

Opinion is divided on the safest way to dispose of them. Throughout England, some were adamant that burning the festive decorations was the only thing to do, although there were further differences over when exactly this burning should take place. Some said this should be done the day before Candlemas on 2nd February, but others believed it should be earlier, on the morning of the 5th or 6th of January. A late nineteenth-century Shropshire belief stated that throwing them outside should be avoided at all costs as it would mean a death in the house before Christmas came round again, and so they should be burnt instead. In Wales, it was said that on the morning after the Twelfth Night, all holly and mistletoe from the Christmas period should be burnt, and any other method of disposal was terribly unlucky.

Others were equally determined about not burning the decorations; some saying that it was a sin to do so. In some areas of Shrewsbury, England and Montgomeryshire, Wales, burning them was said to be unlucky. In Ayrshire, Scotland, it was also said to be bad luck to burn the greenery. Another belief was that if holly were burnt then a death would take place in the following 12 months. A Welsh tradition was to take the evergreens down at Candlemas, but keep them a little longer. They were then burnt in the fire on Shrove Tuesday where pancakes were made; this was also practiced in the Isle of Man. In mid-twentieth-century Shropshire, the remains of the greenery were fed to cattle on Candlemas day for good luck.

FINDING A FOUR-LEAF CLOVER

Perhaps one of the most common symbols associated with good luck, the four-leaf clover is considered lucky across the globe, with this particular superstition popular throughout Europe, the US, Australia and Japan.

As early as the sixteenth century, written references can be found of the luck associated with the four-leafed trefoil or four-leafed grass, with the belief that finding one and keeping it would bring an individual riches all their life long. Another similar belief stated that finding one would lead to the lucky person discovering something good not long after.

Finding a four-leaf clover has been said to bring particular luck in racing and gambling, and to mean that a witch cannot harm the person in possession of one. Such benefits only applied, however, if the clover was carried constantly. If the person showed it to anyone or rashly gave it away, then it was thought that the luck would end immediately. Four-leaf clovers have often been strewn before a new bride, to bring luck to her path.

Another belief holds that finding a four-leaf clover will mean meeting your true lover soon after. In mid-twentieth century Norfolk, England, it was said that four-leafed clovers only grew where a mare had birthed her first foal, whereas an Essex rhyme stated that "if you find a four-leaved clover, all your trouble will be over".

In Ireland, the four-leafed clover is known as the shamrock, a particularly potent symbol of good fortune and much coveted. In Germany, it is popular to give clover charms or items with a clover on them as New Year's Eve presents.

It is said that Eve took a four-leaf clover with her when she was expelled from the Garden of Eden as a reminder of what she had lost. The four leaves have variously been associated with faith, hope, love and luck, or the holy trinity and the grace of God, with a strong link historically to Christian and pre-Christian belief alike.

Four-leaf clovers have also been linked with fairies – possessing one was said to enable a person to see the fairy folk, and also to see through their enchantments.

SEEING A HAY WAGON

72

The image of a cart or wagon carrying hay conjures up images for some of rural harmony from days gone by, with farm workers pulling together to bring in the harvest. In more recent times, the sight might be less familiar, but if you do happen to see a hay cart, be aware that according to some, seeing moving hay might influence your luck.

In Wales, seeing a load of hay was considered good luck, but with one important caveat: if you saw it disappear over a hill or round a corner, then bad luck would come to you instead. According to some, just seeing the back of the wagon is enough to turn your luck. One antidote was to spit and then touch leather for good luck to be restored. Another apparent remedy involved making horns with your fingers as the cart passed.

In Essex, England, it was believed that you should make a wish upon seeing a hay cart. The wish would come true as long as you didn't see the back of the cart as it passed by.

Hay wagons also feature in superstitions in the US, with making a wish on moving hay still a popular practice today. In Kentucky, it was believed you should make a wish, count to 13, then be careful to turn away and not look at the hay wagon again. Indeed, it was bad luck *not* to make a wish; sickness or even death in the family would apparently result if a wish was not made. In Napa, California, it was said that you should make a wish and not look back until the cart was out of sight. It was also said that you should lick the end of your thumb and then make a wish as it dries.

For some, the outcome all depends on which way the cart is going. If it is coming towards you, it is considered good luck, while if it's travelling away – especially if you see it turn off the road – it signals bad fortune ahead.

In Italy, seeing a hay wagon is a good sign, and is said to mean that financial gain is in the near future.

Lightning can be both a majestic and terrifying force of nature, and an electrical storm is a stark reminder of how small we are in the face of such power. The odds of being struck by lightning are relatively slim – around one in 500,000. Despite this, there are still many ideas – some reputable, others less so – on how to avoid being part of that particular statistic.

One superstition from the Philippines is that wearing red clothing during a lightning storm is to be avoided at all costs, as it could apparently lead to you being electrocuted. This belief is also found in Madagascar and Turkey. This is because the colour red is thought to attract lightning. And in Japan and Belgium, picking poppies is thought to cause lightning – another link to the colour red. There is no scientific basis for this belief, however, or that any one colour over another could attract lightning.

Red skies, however, are another matter. According to the old shepherding adage, red is only bad luck at the start of the day, when they predict bad weather ahead. If the sky is red in the evening, then fair weather can be expected the day after.

"Red sky at night, shepherds' delight.
Red sky in the morning, shepherds' warning."

In some parts of the US, it is believed that you should never take a shower during an electrical storm, otherwise electrocution is likely. You also shouldn't turn on the television or talk on the phone, just in case. Another commonly held belief is that lightning occurring in the north will mean that rain is to follow in the near future.

There is also considerable debate regarding which trees offer the best protection from lightning if you happen to be caught out in a storm. Some say that the mighty oak brings the best protection, but others favour holly. Another belief was that placing the remains of a burnt yule log under the bed would protect the house against a lightning strike. According to French lore, charred stone or wood from a lightning strike can have healing properties if placed on an open wound.

HEARING THREE KNOCKS

74

Many things, including bad events, are said to come in threes. One superstitious belief, popular in the UK and the US, links the number three to a negative outcome. It is said that if you hear three knocks that appear to have no cause, then you had better prepare yourself, as something bad is going to happen.

The most common outcome associated with hearing three knocks is a death in the family or of a friend. In England, from at least the eighteenth century, hearing three knocks against the headboard of a person who was sick in bed was taken as an omen of impending death, and many anecdotal stories exist that people believe support this claim. It wasn't only knocks on the bed that it was thought you should be wary of – three such knocks on the door, walls or even outside the window, were also considered an omen of death.

The belief that three knocks heralded a death was still going strong in the twentieth century. Generally the knocks were said to come before the death occurred, but there were also instances of the knocks sounding afterwards, in the home of friends or family who lived a distance away.

What happened if only two knocks were heard? In such instances, all was not lost; the ill person was in danger, but could still recover, unless three knocks were then heard. Linked to this superstition was the belief that when ghosts visited they announced themselves with three knocks.

A variation of this superstition is that three knocks might simply be a warning of impending bad luck rather than a death. The three might also be a clue as to when such an event might occur, whether it be three days, three weeks, three months or even three years in the future.

KNITTING OUTSIDE

75

With the first knitted items in existence dating from Egypt between 1000 and 1400AD, the practice of knitting has a long and varied provenance. As both a profitable economy and a popular past time, interest in knitting has seen a resurgence in recent years, with people of all ages reaching for their needles to produce all manner of wonderful creations. Before you sit down for a knitting session however, make sure you are not doing something that could have unforeseen consequences.

According to superstition in Iceland, if you are struck by the urge to knit outside it is best not to give into temptation, especially during the colder months. Knitting outside is said to prolong winter, meaning a longer wait before fairer weather returns. Therefore it might be a good idea to stay indoors to knit instead – not a bad idea if it is icy outside!

Another popular knitting-related superstition is that of the curse of the love sweater. According to this "sweater curse", knitting a sweater for a loved one is a recipe for disaster, as giving it to them will mean your relationship will soon end. This superstition is held in several areas of the world, so perhaps it might be best to give your significant other a different gift instead. A similar superstition is that knitting a pair of socks for a lover will lead to them walking away from you.

Knitting needles should never be passed between friends for fear of stabbing or puncturing the relationship. They should be set down by one person and picked up by the other. Starting a new knitting project on a Friday is also frowned upon, as is knitting for a baby before it is born, as both are said to lead to bad luck.

In Latvia, if you want the warmest, highest quality socks and mittens, they should be knitted in summer, ready for the cold months ahead.

DROPPING CUTLERY

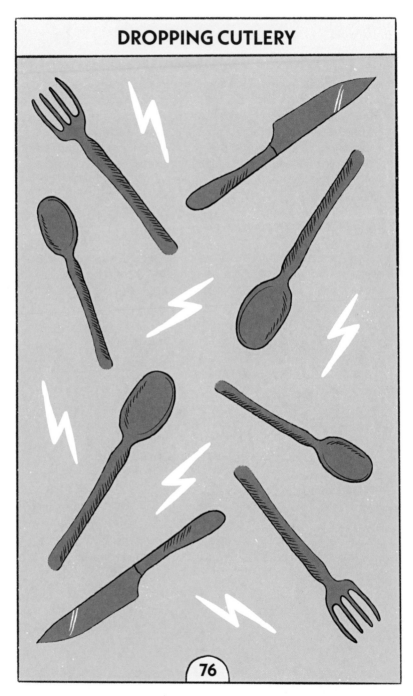

Dropping things is an almost unavoidable nuisance in life, and as we have already seen, there are many superstitious beliefs surrounding what happens when we drop certain things. According to many, dropped cutlery is something to watch out for, as it is said that the dropping of a piece of cutlery or a utensil can foretell the arrival of visitors to your door.

There were variations of this superstition across time and location, but in general, according to nineteenth- and twentieth-century English belief, dropping cutlery meant visitors were to be expected. If a knife was dropped then the visitor would be a man; if it was a fork, then a woman would come to call. In addition, if a spoon happened to fall, then it signified a child visiting soon. This was similarly believed in Ireland.

In the US, some said that if a fork or a knife was dropped then a man would visit, while a spoon suggested a female visitor. In eighteenth-century Kentucky, US, a knife meant a woman would visit, a fork meant a man, while a fork could also mean a best friend would arrive. In addition, a tablespoon signified a woman and baby, and a large spoon meant a large family.

In the Philippines, a dropped fork signified the arrival of a man, and a spoon a woman. Variations elsewhere include a fork for a boy, a teaspoon for a young girl, and a tablespoon for a woman. Some believed that the direction the item pointed after it fell could give the additional information of which direction the visitors would come from. It could also mean which way good luck was coming from.

According to belief in Radnor, Wales, there was the interesting addition to the more well-known versions that if a carving knife was dropped, it meant a policeman was coming!

Another belief regarding dropping cutlery involves who should pick it up. According to superstition, picking it up yourself is asking for bad luck, so it is best to find someone else to do it for you!

LUCKY CHIMNEY SWEEP

A fond memory from childhood for many is that of the chimney sweep scene from Disney's *Mary Poppins*. Although under fire in recent years due to claims of racism in the original source material, the image of the sweep itself has long been seen as a positive symbol across many areas of Europe, and is a sign of good luck.

Sweeps are considered good luck in Hungary, Germany and much of Eastern Europe. In the Czech Republic, they are literally seen as human good luck charms. When a sweep is seen, touching them or touching one of your own buttons and making a wish are common practice. The figure of the lucky sweep is likewise prominent in Poland, and grabbing your button to make a wish is a must. To gain the most luck, however, you would need to spot a sweep, a priest and a white horse in a row!

According to one enduring legend, the origin of the sweep as good luck goes back to the eighteenth century. As the story goes, George III of England (or George II, depending on which version you listen to) found himself in a sticky situation when his horse was spooked and bolted; a courageous chimney sweep saved the day and the grateful monarch declared that sweeps were good luck, and made the fact a royal decree.

In England and Ireland, there was a practice of bowing or curtseying to a sweep or taking your hat off to them, to attract good luck. Wishing a sweep "good morning" was also considered lucky. Luck would also increase with the number of sweeps seen together at one time – the more sweeps, the more luck you would have.

It was considered very lucky to see a sweep on your wedding day, and some sweeps made a pretty penny charging for their attendance at weddings and to kiss the bride to be! Be careful, however, as seeing the back of a sweep on your wedding day was said to bring bad luck. On the day of the wedding of Elizabeth II and Prince Philip, the groom shook hands with a sweep outside Kensington Palace, for good luck.

UNLUCKY PRESIDENT MENEM

78

We've covered a lot of unlucky objects and actions so far, but what about unlucky people? An Argentine superstition surrounding the late, controversial former President, Carlos Saúl Menem, states that he was a very unlucky person to be around indeed.

President for a decade, from July 1989 to December 1999, Menem was and still is regarded by many in Argentina as *mufa* – very bad luck. Various calamities are laid at his door. It is said that his bad luck was responsible for powerboat racing champion Daniel Scioli losing an arm in a boat crash in 1989 after Menem shook his hand. The stagnation of Gabriela Sabatini's tennis career is likewise attributed to her rashly playing a game with the president. Two politicians Menem appointed after his election died soon after. In the 1990 World Cup, the Argentine goalkeeper broke his kneecap soon after a misplaced pat on the knee from the president when trying to shake his hand. Whether these instances are true or not, Menem's association with bad luck persisted, even being linked to the San Andreas fault earthquake in 1989 and the economic crisis in Argentina of 2001. An avid sports fan, Menem was banned from attending Atletico River Plate football matches for fear he would adversely affect the outcome of his favourite team. It is said that even Menem himself believed that a spell or a curse had been worked against him.

According to superstition, it is bad luck to even mention the man's name. People say Mendem or Mendez instead when referring to him. Is there any way to undo the Menem curse? If you are careless enough to utter his name, a man should touch his left testicle with his right hand and a woman should touch her left breast in order to avoid the bad luck that would otherwise follow.

It was not always doom and gloom though, and when British Queen Elizabeth II met Menem in 1998, no ill effects were reported.

HICCUPS

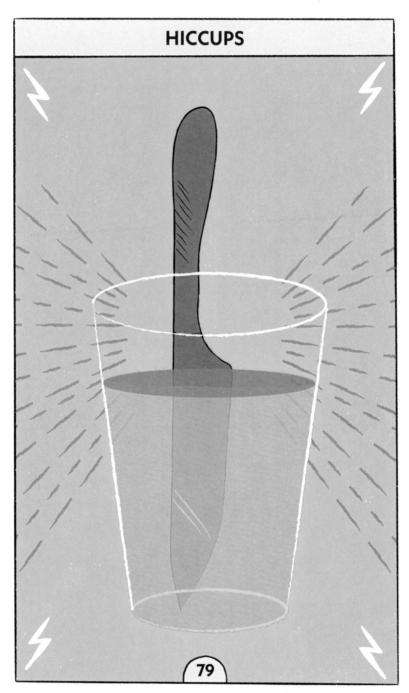

79

Hiccups are a common and irritating affliction, often hitting at the least favourable moment. From childhood, we all no doubt remember being told of various supposed remedies for this uncomfortable condition, from the mundane holding your breath to the more challenging drinking a glass of water upside down. According to superstition, however, what exactly do hiccups mean?

Sometimes hiccups have negative connotations. According to superstition in India, having hiccups – either continuously or just one bout – could mean that someone is thinking bad things about you. It can also apparently mean that someone is simply remembering you at that moment, so it's best not to jump to conclusions.

In Russia, having hiccups is likewise a sign that someone is thinking about you or missing you. Some say that if you list your friends and associates in your head, whichever name you reach when the hiccups stop is the one who is thinking about you. This is generally seen as a good thing, as it is said that the person is thinking good things about you. In Hungary, having hiccups can mean that someone is talking about you. In Romania, it is likewise said that hiccups show someone is thinking – or speaking – about you. It is thought that the hiccups will continue, until you guess the name of the person in question.

There are many varied cures available for when the hiccups strike. An old English cure advised spitting on the forefinger of your right hand, making a cross on the front of your left shoe, and reciting the Lord's Prayer backwards. In the Philippines, wetting a small piece of paper towel and sticking it to your forehead is said to do the trick. In Norway, it is said that you should place a knife in a glass and then take three sips of the water.

In Columbia, hiccups are considered dangerous and some say that you can die from them. But if you place a small piece of wet paper on your forehead in between the eyebrows, then it is thought that they should subside. There is also a superstition in Japan that says if you hiccup 100 times in a row, then you will die.

THE FIRST BUTTERFLY OF THE YEAR

80

The sight of a butterfly fluttering past is one of the wonders of the warmer months of the year, from the resplendent Red Admiral to the modest Cabbage White. In the wealth of folklore attached to these flighty creatures, great importance is placed on the first butterfly that you see in the year. Make sure you note the colour of the first one you see, as according to many, it might have an influence on the months ahead.

According to English superstition, if the first butterfly you see in the year is white, then all will be well – this means you will eat white bread, which, during the late nineteenth century, was synonymous with good luck. If the first butterfly spied happens to be brown, however, it is best to be wary, since that signifies brown bread and corresponding bad luck for the year ahead.

In Brazil, white butterflies are also considered lucky. If the first butterfly you see in the year is white, then the year ahead is thought to be prosperous and filled with good luck.

Seeing a white butterfly first is also considered lucky in Ireland. White butterflies are said to be the souls of children that have passed. This belief is also held in Germany, and in Japan, white butterflies are likewise said to be the souls of the departed. In the Philippines, Central America and China, butterflies are thought to be a sign of a deceased friend or relative making contact.

According to another superstition, thankfully no longer popular, it was said that the first butterfly seen in the year should be killed. To not do so was thought in some places to bring bad luck for the year to come.

Generally, black and dark butterflies are seen as bad signs. They are often seen as a bad omen, predicting death or bad fortune ahead.

LIGHTING A CIGARETTE FROM A CANDLE

81

Although the negative health impacts of smoking are well known today, the tobacco industry has long been a thriving one, and there was a time when smoking cigarettes was the fashionable norm for many. According to one still popular superstition, if you do choose to light up, be careful what you use – if you use a candle to light your cigarette, it is said that you risk killing a sailor.

This superstition is common across Northern and Eastern Europe, and lighting a cigarette from a candle is considered taboo in many areas. This is a popular superstition in Germany, where either a sailor or, in some versions, an angel, is said to die if a cigarette is lit from a candle. There is apparently a way to avert this consequence, however: knock on the table and the sailor or angel should be safe. This superstition is also prevalent in Iceland, where along with the implied danger to a sailor, it is considered rude to light three cigarettes from the same candle.

The exact origins of this superstition are unknown. According to some, it dates back to a time when the livelihood of a sailor was not as certain as it is today, and one way a sailor could supplement his income was to make and sell matches. Therefore, if you lit your cigarette from a candle, or so the story goes, you would not be using or buying as many matches, and therefore depriving a sailor of money, and in extreme cases, causing him to starve. Although times became more stable, the superstition still lives on.

In Russia, in recent years there have been several cases of people facing prosecution for lighting cigarettes from church candles, due to the religious offence caused by this act.

UNLUCKY REDHEADS

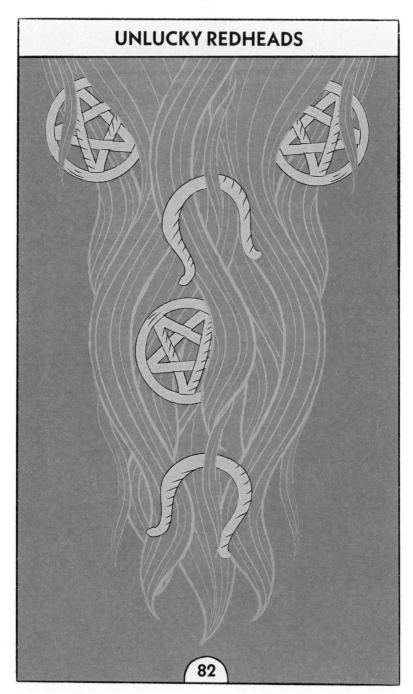

82

Hair comes in a wide array of fascinating colours and shades. It seems, however, that out of all of these, red shades have most consistently received an undeservedly bad reputation throughout history. Those with red hair have, by extension, been both revered and reviled, but the general consensus is that red-haired individuals bring with them a lot of bad luck.

Red hair has long been linked with treachery and an artful, deceptive personality. Evident in the fifteenth century was the link between those with red hair and foxes, which were also said to have these less than desirable personality traits. A traveller in the nineteenth century observed that a deep prejudice existed against those with red hair in all the areas of England that he visited. It was also thought that a red-headed child was a sign of a mother's infidelity and they were therefore seen to be unlucky.

It was generally considered bad luck if the first person seen on a journey was a redhead. According to Irish superstition, if you met a red-haired woman first thing in the morning then you could expect a bad day ahead. In Scotland and elsewhere, seeing a red-headed person on the way to sea or having a red-haired person on board meant that a bad day's fishing was ahead. According to some, bees will sting a redhead more than people with hair of another colour. Red-haired individuals were also considered unlucky to have in the house on New Year's Day; if a red-haired man was the first person through the door on New Year's Day then it was said that there would be a death in the house before the year was out.

In Poland, it is thought that passing three redheads in a row is greatly auspicious, and you will win the lottery. In New Zealand, red hair is considered lucky, and likewise in Germany it is seen as a good thing to have a child with red hair. In recent years, there have been several gatherings around the world to celebrate all that is wonderful about having red hair. The largest event, the Redhead Day festival, which has been held in the Netherlands since 2005, welcomes visitors from over 80 countries and takes place over three days.

AN ITCHY NOSE

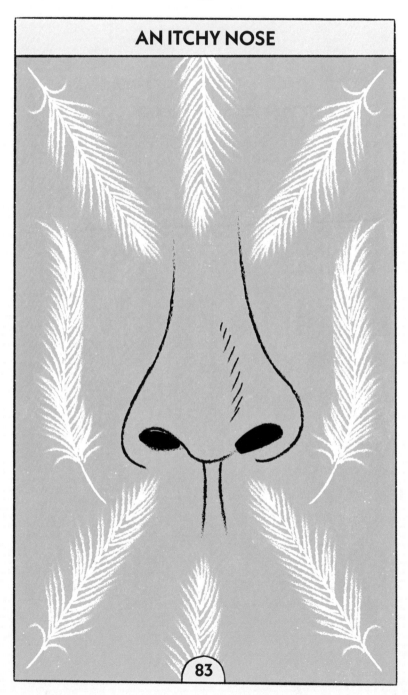

83

Random itches and strange feelings throughout the body are frequently featured in superstitions, and are often said to predict events to come. The nose is no exception. When your nose has a tickle, are you just getting a cold? Possibly not. An itchy nose is another occurrence that, according to superstition, can provide revealing details about the future.

A popular belief across the world states that if your nose is itchy you can expect a visitor or visitors. Some say that you can even predict who will visit – if the left side of your nose itches, then the visitor will be male; if it is the right side with a tickle, then a woman is to be expected.

In Ireland, an itchy nose is said to predict a fight; the fight can be avoided, however, if someone slaps your hand and you do the same in return, or if some other form of mock fight takes place in lieu of a more violent one. In Romania, superstition also says that if your nose itches then you can expect a fight or violence from someone soon. Some believe that saying *Doamne Fereste!* – God Forbid – three times will prevent this from occurring.

British superstition had various suggestions for what an itchy nose might mean. In the seventeenth century, the arrival of guests or drinking wine could be on the cards, depending on who and when you asked. Throughout the eighteenth and nineteenth centuries, the most common beliefs were that an itchy nose would mean you would kiss a fool, drink wine, be vexed or receive bad news. In the Scottish Highlands, a stranger or a letter were said to be due. The drinking connection continued into the twentieth century, where it was said that you would drink with strangers, be kissed, cursed, vexed or shake hands with a fool. Running into a gatepost was another potential consequence after an itchy nose, as was getting a surprise or being angry.

GOING HOME AFTER A FUNERAL

84

There are many superstitions relating to one of humankind's biggest preoccupations and fears – death. Funeral traditions vary and are celebrated differently across the world, but despite this, there are several similarities between the superstitions linked to them, particularly regarding what to do when returning home after a funeral or wake.

Across Europe and elsewhere, it is believed that mourners shouldn't return home via the same route that the funeral procession took on its outward journey. Instead, those returning from the funeral should take a different route home. This was very important, as it was believed this would prevent the ghost of the departed from following them. To make certain, it was also advised to take a more meandering, winding route, to confuse the spirit further.

In the Philippines, it is also considered bad luck to go straight home after a funeral. Doing so apparently runs the risk of death following you back to your house – so be sure to stop off somewhere on your way, just in case.

On a similar note, in Yorkshire, England, the furniture in the bedroom of the deceased would be changed after the funeral party left; this was to prevent the ghost from recognizing the room if it returned and decided to stay. It was also generally believed that if the dead were not carried out feet first, then there was a risk that the ghost would return.

It is generally accepted that if you meet a funeral procession, you should turn back and walk with it for a certain distance or number of steps in order to avoid bad luck or your own death. Taking your hat off upon seeing a funeral procession was always considered to be advisable, either for good luck, or to stop the spirits from being angered. There was also a belief in England and Ireland, among other countries, that whichever gender you met on the way to a funeral, a person of that sex would be the next to die.

BURNING LOST TEETH

85

Losing a tooth, especially that all-important first one, is a milestone in every child's life. It does leave one vital question, however – what exactly should be done with the tooth when it is no longer needed?

One popular idea was that any tooth that had fallen out or been extracted, should be burned. This belief was in existence in England from at least the seventeenth century, when it was advised to either wrap the tooth or put salt around it before burning. A nineteenth-century belief suggested that if the tooth was not burned and an animal found it and ate it, then the unfortunate person would have their new tooth grow back not as a human tooth, but like the tooth of the animal that had eaten it. Sometimes a rhyme would be recited as the tooth was burned, a popular one was:

"Fire, fire, burn a bone, God send me another tooth again; A straight one, a white one, and in the same place."

Burning teeth was also popular across Europe. Another reason for this was the belief that if a witch got hold of your old tooth then they could use it to work bad magic and have power over you. Burying teeth was another solution, with the hope that new teeth would grow like strong plants.

In Devon, England, teeth were not disposed of but were instead kept; they had to be carefully hidden, however, in case a dog or an enemy found them, which could have disastrous consequences.

In some Asian countries, including China, Korea, India and Japan, there was a practice of throwing teeth either upwards onto the roof if it was a bottom tooth, or downwards onto the floor if it was a top tooth. This was to encourage the new tooth to grow in the right direction. In some central Asian countries, however, baby teeth were placed in fat and actually fed to dogs. This was so that the new teeth would come through as strong as the teeth of a dog.

A SEVENTH CHILD

7

A significant number the world over, seven has long been said to be imbued with all manner of mystical and important qualities. According to belief in several areas, a seventh-born child is someone very special indeed, in possession of various psychic or healing gifts.

Originally, it was specifically seventh sons that were considered to be imbued with special powers; this was even more so if their father was also a seventh son. It was important that these were seven consecutive sons, with no daughters breaking up the line in between, although later the association was also extended to seven consecutive daughters. In Scotland, it was said that the seventh daughter of a seventh daughter would possess the gift of second sight.

In sixteenth-century England, it was popularly believed that a seventh son could cure scrofula – tuberculosis of the neck – by the simple power of touch. By the eighteenth century, this healing ability extended to all manner of other ailments. According to Irish belief, the saliva of a seventh son had the ability to heal. In France, such a seventh son was known as a *marcou* and could likewise cure scrofula, which was also known as the "king's evil", deriving from the belief that the royal touch could cure this disease. With a *fleur-de-lys* shaped mark on their body, the patient would either touch this symbol, or the *marcou* would breathe on it to affect the cure. Another popular belief was that a seventh son was likely to become a doctor, their healing powers putting them in good stead for that profession.

A less positive association comes from Romanian superstition, where it is said that seventh sons are particularly prone to becoming *strigoi* – vampires.

In Argentina, it is believed that a seventh son is particularly susceptible to becoming a *lobison* or werewolf. The fear of werewolves in the nineteenth century was so strong that some seventh sons were even murdered. Unrelated to this is the tradition of the Argentinian president standing as a godparent to seventh sons, a practice dating from 1907 that is said to have originated in Tzarist Russia. It was not until the 1970s that seventh daughters also became eligible for this privilege.

THREE ON A MATCH

Another superstition relating to the lighting of cigarettes is that of lighting three cigarettes with a single match. Dating from the nineteenth or early twentieth century, according to this belief, if three cigarettes were lit from the same match, then the third person to have theirs lit would die.

This superstition has its origins in the military, and initially referred specifically to soldiers lighting a smoke. According to the superstition, lighting the first cigarette would alert the enemy to the light, on the second being lit, the enemy would take aim, and the third cigarette lighting would provide the light by which the enemy would fire, thus killing the unlucky man holding it.

It is unclear exactly when this superstition originated. It is sometimes suggested that it originated during the 1920s. According to this theory, Ivar Kreuger, Swedish match-making magnate, exploited the existing superstition to encourage the use of more matches, which was obviously good for business. However, queries over the origins of this superstition were around as early as 1916, so it was already entrenched by then. One suggestion was that it came from the Boer War: 1899-1902. It was said that there had been enough occasions of the third man to take a light being shot directly afterwards that the negative association was made.

In late twentieth-century Essex, it was said that you should never offer someone a match three times. Another explanation believed by some is that it comes from Russia; three altar candles are lit from the same taper in the funeral ritual. Doing the same for smoking is impious and unlucky. The belief is also mentioned in a late nineteenth-century Mexican source – it was said that bad luck would be the fate of the third man if three men lit their cigarettes from the same match.

There are many references to this superstition in film, television, songs and books throughout the twentieth and twenty-first centuries, and it remains popular today.

COVERING MIRRORS

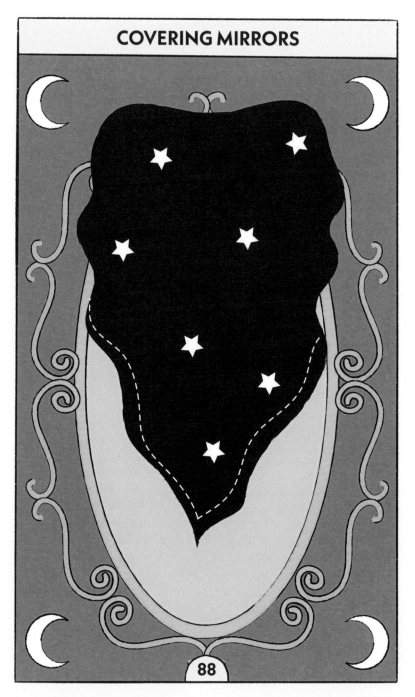

88

Mirrors and what is reflected in them is a preoccupation of many superstitions the world over. A common mirror-related superstition is the practice of covering a mirror, which usually takes place when someone is ill, when there has been a death or even during a thunderstorm. This superstition is widespread across the world in a wealth of variations.

When a death occurs, it is common for mirrors to be covered or turned towards the wall. In some cases, it is any reflective surface, which includes paintings and even framed pictures. Some say that the covering should be done at the moment of death, while others say that it should be done while the person is sick as it is considered unlucky for them to see their reflection in a mirror.

In China, there are several reasons for covering a mirror after someone has died. One is the belief that if someone sees the coffin reflected in the glass then there will be further death in the family. Another is that the spirit of the departed would be distressed to see their reflection and realise that they had become a ghost.

One common belief was that to look in the mirror in the room where someone had died brought the risk of seeing the corpse – or the devil – reflected in the mirror behind them. Another common belief was that if the dead saw themselves in a mirror, they would be confused and either unable or unwilling to then carry on to the spirit world and would instead remain on Earth.

The practice of covering mirrors has gone on for centuries in cultures across the world, due to the long-held superstition connecting mirrors and death. In many areas of Europe, mirrors were covered with white cloth, although black was also sometimes used. In the US, at President Abraham Lincoln's funeral in 1865, the frames were draped with black, while the glass itself was covered with white.

DISPOSING OF HAIR CUTTINGS

89

Whether you've just had a trim or gone for a whole change of style, having your hair cut leaves varying amounts of cut hair that is no longer required. At the hairdressers, they sweep it up and you don't give it another thought. According to superstition, however, it is said that considerable care needs to be taken when getting rid of those unwanted locks.

One reason for being so careful about what happened to discarded hair was the belief that if someone had possession of a hair – or something else from your body, such as nail clippings – then someone could use them to do you harm through sympathetic magic. Witches were often accused of using the hairs from a victim to do great harm.

In Britain, it was also believed that if hair cuttings were left then birds would use them to make a nest. This might sound like a good idea for the birds, but for the previous owner of the hair the outcome would not be so favourable. It was thought that as the birds twisted the hair tightly into their nest, the person would suffer from a terrible headache. The outcome would be particularly bad if the bird happened to be a magpie.

The best way to avoid any of these unwanted outcomes was to sweep the hair away and then burn it to make sure nobody could get their hands on it and use it for nefarious purposes. It was considered bad luck to just throw the hair away.

Contrary to this idea was the Irish belief that hair shouldn't be burned, but should be buried or kept safe somewhere else instead. This was because on Resurrection Day, a person would need all their hair to stand before God.

A Dutch belief states that you can use a lock of hair to find out how long your life will be. Cut a lock and set fire to it: if it burns for a long time then you will live for at least 70 years. A short burn? Well, it's just a superstition, isn't it?

BORN WITH TEETH

90

Babies are usually born with empty gums, but in rare cases – between one in 2,000 to one in 3,500 cases, some are born with one or even two teeth, generally the central incisor. These natal teeth, as they are known, have been regarded with suspicion and reverence throughout history, and there are several superstitions attached to this phenomenon.

As early as 77AD, Roman scholar Pliny the Elder writes of how babies born with a tooth were considered special. He gives examples of distinguished men who were born with a tooth, but warns that if the child happens to be female then these unexpected teeth were a very bad sign of things to come.

Opinion has been divided across the globe since then regarding whether a baby being born with teeth is an auspicious sign or cause for alarm. According to some, being born with teeth could mean that the child would be lucky in life, and also that they would possess great intelligence. On the other end of the spectrum, being born with teeth was said to lead to becoming a murderer in later life, or that the child was born to be hanged. In some areas, it was believed that babies having teeth at birth would bring bad luck to the communities in which they lived, whereas in others the early teeth would bring good fortune to those they lived among.

Cutting teeth early – known as neonatal teeth – was also seen to be special. It could mean that the child would have siblings soon. A Lancashire saying stated "Soon with goom [gum], quick with woom [womb]," meaning that more babies would be on the way soon if a child cut their teeth early. Early teeth were, however, also sometimes linked with an early death. If the first teeth came through at the top, this was thought to be a sign of a short life; if the bottom teeth came first, however, then the family could breathe a sigh of relief, as this apparently meant that the child would have many years ahead of them.

A TOAD CROSSING YOUR PATH

91

Toads have received bad press over the centuries, and are often linked to dark and unfavourable places, witchcraft and black magic. Often said to spit at people, toads were also associated with poison and disease. What does superstition say about meeting one of these often maligned creatures? It might not all be as bad as you might think.

In nineteenth-century Edinburgh, Scotland, it was considered good luck if a toad went across the path that a bride was going to take. In early twentieth-century Devon, England, however, it was said that terrible misfortune would befall either the bride or groom if they were to see a toad. In Somerset, it was generally considered good luck for a toad to cross your path. But care needed to be taken not to frighten it, as if it hopped away, then it was believed that death would surely follow you. It could be unlucky for a toad to walk across your foot, but it was thought that spitting would avert any potential calamity.

In the US, seeing a toad could have various meanings. One was that rain was on the way. It could also signal impending bad luck, that you would stub your toe or there would be a death in the family. Seeing a toad was also linked to a cow's milk going dry.

Often linked to witchcraft, a toad in the house could be unlucky and a sign that a curse had been placed on the household. Toads were therefore removed carefully for fear of angering witches. Some believed that killing the toad would break its hold over you. It could also, however, be lucky to have a toad in the house, and getting rid of one could bring bad luck to the entire family for the year ahead.

Toads are also symbols of good luck and prosperity in some cultures. Meeting a toad was sometimes said to have monetary benefits, predicting that money would soon come your way. Toads were popular choices in folk cures for various ailments, including whooping cough, epilepsy and warts. In Scotland, rubbing a sprained wrist with a live toad was said to cure it.

A LUCKY SILVER COIN

92

Silver has been associated with protection and healing for centuries, and is said to aid against several ailments and misfortunes. Silver coins are thought to be particularly lucky, featuring in a whole range of superstitions.

A popular wedding tradition involved the bride putting a silver coin in her shoe for good luck. Dating from the nineteenth century is the popular rhyme: "Something old, something new, something borrowed, something blue, and a silver sixpence in her shoe." The coin was said to bring the bride good luck on her wedding day and beyond. In Scotland, a groom would put a silver sixpence in his shoe to avoid being cursed by a disappointed rival. Also in Scotland, a woman who had turned down several suitors was advised to wear a piece of silver in one shoe to avoid the wrath of those she had rejected. In Sweden, the bride receives a gold coin from her mother for her right shoe and a silver one from her father for her left, so that she is never without money.

Putting a silver sixpence in the Christmas pudding mixture is another popular practice. Whoever is served the portion with the coin is said to have good luck for the year ahead. Likewise, some make a loaf on New Year's Day with a silver coin baked inside. Whoever finds the coin in their slice will apparently have a prosperous year.

In Lithuania, guests scatter coins on the dance floor before the newlyweds have their first dance. One of these coins has the bride and groom's initials on it. After the dance, the coins are collected up and placed in a jar, and whoever picks out the initialled coin gets to have a dance with either the bride or the groom.

A silver sixpence in your pocket is also a popular practice to ensure success in an exam, while a silver coin buried under the threshold when a house is built, is said to bring good luck. According to folklore, using a silver sixpence as a bullet would kill those that are otherwise immune to lead bullets, such as witches and werewolves.

SEEING A SHOOTING STAR

93

There are many of us who scour the night sky for the sight of a shooting star. Not really stars at all, the distinctive momentary streak is caused when a meteoroid enters the earth's atmosphere, a flash that it is easy to blink and miss. If you do happen to spy one, however, there are several superstitions connected to this phenomenon.

The belief that falling stars are significant is almost universal. One popular belief is that when one falls it announces that a birth has taken place, or even shows where the baby has been born. The "star" is said to be the soul of the new child descending from heaven.

A less positive connection is the belief that a shooting or falling star signifies a death or some other disaster. According to this belief, each shooting star is a soul ascending to heaven. Some suggest that a falling star could also mean that someone is dying at that moment. Seeing a shooting star was also sometimes believed to be an omen that someone would die soon. If the star was accompanied by an audible noise, then the death would apparently be someone of great importance.

Wishing on a falling star is another popular past-time. If you make a wish when you see a star falling and you complete the wish before the star disappears, then it is said to come true. Are you experiencing financial difficulties? Next time you see a shooting star, say "money" three times. If you manage this before the star vanishes, then it is said that your wish will come true.

It is advisable to pay attention to which direction the star is falling. If the star falls on the right it is said to mean good luck, but on the left, it is considered a bad sign and you should prepare for bad times ahead.

Other ideas regarding shooting stars include the belief that seeing one means someone will soon marry. Sightings are even thought to act as a cure for bad skin. If you hold a cloth to your face as the star falls, some believe that the ailment will be cleared.

PICKING UP A HANDKERCHIEF

94

According to superstition, you should be careful if you happen to drop your handkerchief. If you pick it up yourself, it is said to bring you bad luck. Instead, make sure that someone else picks it up for you, and all will be well. In Belgium, it is said that if you pick your own handkerchief up, you may cry for the whole year to come.

Handkerchiefs are also not considered good gifts for a friend or loved one; this is because gifting them a hanky is said to be giving them tears and many causes to shed them. It is also thought to bring anger and illness – not something you want to risk when you like someone! In the US, it was considered bad luck to lend someone a handkerchief for the same reasons. In Russia, giving a handkerchief as a gift was also said to bring tears. Likewise, a handkerchief used at a funeral should be discarded before returning home; taking it with you risked taking tears into your home. In Sweden, it is advised to never give a lover a handkerchief, as doing so is thought to wipe away their affection for you.

If using a new or newly ironed handkerchief, be wary of putting it straight into your pocket without unfolding it first as this is thought to bring bad luck. Another belief in the US is that finding a handkerchief on the floor means bad news or that a bad letter is coming your way.

Prone to losing things? Next time you can't find something, just tie a knot in your handkerchief and it is said that you will soon be reunited with your missing item. Traditionally, people would tie a knot in their handkerchief to remind themselves that there was something important that should not be forgotten: though the knot couldn't actually tell them what it was that they needed to remember!

CATS PREDICTING THE WEATHER

95

Cats are well known for being intelligent and sensitive creatures, and their ability to respond to changes before they are discernable to the human eye have long been documented. They are credited in particular with the ability to predict the weather and many superstitions exist regarding what the behaviour of your favourite feline might forecast.

In general, if a cat is showing agitation or excitement, then it is said that severe weather could be expected. An eighteenth-century English belief stated that a cat would frisk about when snow or hail was due, and superstition in Wales said that a cat would behave in an erratic fashion before rain. A popular superstition from the nineteenth century stated that if a cat was prancing and jumping about on board a ship, then a storm was on the way: "the cat has a gale of wind in her tail." A cat washing its ears has been seen as a sign of rain from at least the eighteenth century, and if it is done vigorously, strong rain is apparently on the cards.

In Scotland, a cat with its back to the fire is thought to mean that cold or frosty weather is to come. In England, a cat with its back to the fire apparently means rain or cold weather. A cat sitting with its tail towards the fire is generally a bad sign, and is said to predict bad luck. In the US, if a cat has its back to the fire, a cold spell is thought to be on the way.

In Holland, if a cat claws at curtains and carpets, it is said that wind is on the way. In the US, if a cat has all four paws tucked under it while it sleeps, then bad weather is said to be due. Likewise, a cat licking its fur backwards was seen as a warning to prepare for a hailstorm.

In Japan, a cat washing its face meant that visitors should be expected. Visitors were also predicted if a cat wiped the same ear three or more times with one paw.

UNLUCKY GREEN

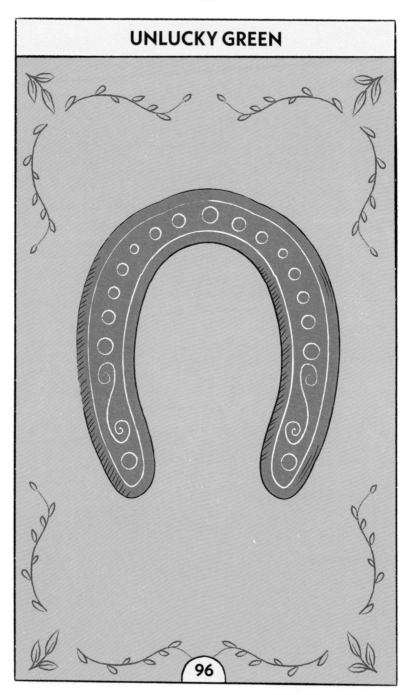

Many colours are believed to be symbolic and have hidden meanings, and these beliefs can differ from country to country. Green is a popular but contradictory colour, linked to fertility, success, wealth and peace on the one hand, and infidelity and jealousy on the other. What does superstition have to say about the colour green?

In China, green is considered to be a lucky colour. Buildings, including restaurants and banks, are often painted green, and the colour has many positive associations such as hope, wealth, fertility, harmony, cleanliness and purity.

In NASCAR racing in the US, green cars have been associated with bad luck and unfortunate crashes since the first half of the twentieth century. It was therefore once considered unlucky to race a green car, but this taboo is not as prevalent today.

Green can also be seen as a dangerous colour due to its connection with the fair folk. It was said to be the colour of choice of the fairies, and according to Scottish and Irish superstition, wearing green, especially on a wedding day, was thought to attract bad luck. The fairies might resent a human wearing their colour for a wedding so much that they might even do harm to the wearer. Regardless of this, green was considered a bad colour to wed in: "They that marry in green, their sorrow is soon seen." In the northern counties of England, this belief was so strong that sometimes all green was banned from weddings – including green vegetables at the meal!

Another belief about green clothes is that wearing them will soon lead to tragedy. According to this superstition, after green comes black, meaning that after wearing green you will soon be wearing black to attend a funeral. Green is also said to be an unlucky colour to dress a baby in.

According to nautical folklore, green boats are unlucky. This is because of the link between the colour green and land; it was believed that a green vessel would therefore be more likely to run aground. Some sailors took no chances, and would not allow anything green on board.

SEWING ON A SUNDAY

97

Long known as the day of rest in some cultures, there are many prohibitions and ideas about what one can and cannot do on a Sunday. One topic on which superstition has much to say is that of sewing: should it be done on a Sunday or will it lead to tears?

A popular superstition in the UK and the US states that sewing on a Sunday is not a good idea. According to this belief, any stitches that are sewn on that day will need to be ripped out using your nose on Monday, or, even worse, when you reach heaven. Depending on how much sewing you do, that could be a lot of stitches! Some say that for each stitch sewn on Sunday, seven will need to be taken out again. It is also believed by some that knitting on a Sunday will have the same outcome. In Wales, it was said that if someone was taken ill when sewing clothing or bed linen on a Sunday, then they would not be able to die until the stitches were unpicked.

A similar superstition is the belief that any work carried out on a Sunday will come undone again on a Monday. It is also said to be unadvisable to start a sewing project on a Friday if you are unable to finish it that same day; it will never be finished otherwise. Some also suggest caution against sewing on a Saturday as this is also bad luck.

Another belief is that sewing shouldn't be done at night. In India, this belief is so entrenched that many shopkeepers refuse to sell needles after 6pm, due to the belief that to do so is an insult to the sun god.

UNLUCKY HARES

98

The hare is frequently referenced in myth, legend and superstition – a magical yet often feared creature that has inspired and repulsed in equal measure throughout history.

According to the Bible, eating hare meat was considered taboo. This prohibition against eating hare was still in place in Britain in 50BC, when it was considered unlawful for Britons to eat them. This negative connotation continued, and in the sixteenth century it was advised to avoid eating hare for fear of getting palsy.

Hares have often been linked to witches and witchcraft; a hare was a popular choice for a witches' familiar, and witches were also often said to be able to shapeshift into this form. In sixteenth-century Ireland, any hare found among the herds on the morning of May Day was said to be a witch and should be destroyed, otherwise it would steal the butter. This belief persisted into the nineteenth century, when hares were still regarded with suspicion.

Hares were also said to be able to predict – or cause – a fire. If one was seen running through a town, it was believed that a fire would happen soon after, with several anecdotal cases keeping this superstition alive.

Meeting a hare or having one cross your path was considered bad luck. It was said to be particularly bad luck for a bride if a hare crossed her path, and she should expect bad times ahead. Many people would turn back home after a hare crossed their path, and in particular many fishermen would not go out to sea if a hare crossed their path on the way to their vessel. The very word "hare" has been considered bad luck – fishermen very often avoided saying the word, especially when they were out at sea.

A hare's foot on the other hand, was considered to be good luck. Roman scholar Pliny the elder suggested carrying a hare's foot as a cure for gout. Later superstition stated that if the right foot from a hare was carried around in your pocket, it would protect against rheumatism or witchcraft.

PEACOCK FEATHERS

The peacock is one of the most majestic birds in appearance; the distinctive eye pattern on its feathers is reproduced in fabric, jewellery and decorations the world over. Opinion is divided, however, regarding the impact these splendid creatures have on our lives – are peacock feathers good or bad luck?

In general, across the western world, peacock feathers are considered to be bad luck. In England, having peacock feathers in the house was said to be very bad luck indeed: misfortune of all kinds was believed to be caused by their presence, from general losses to illness and death. Some said that the household would not have luck again until the feathers were removed. This negative connection was so deep that people were at times incited to extreme reactions, such as tearing the feather from a visitor's hat or even boxing someone's ears for having brought peacock feathers into the house.

Another belief was that peacock feathers kept in the house would result in any unmarried women living there never marrying. It was particularly frowned upon to place peacock feathers in a nursery or child's bedroom.

Peacock feathers were also considered taboo in the theatre world, and many would not allow them on stage in any form. It was said that great misfortune and accidents would occur if they were present.

The peacock itself was said to be able to predict rain: "When the peacock loudly bawls, soon you'll have both rain and squalls." They could also apparently predict a death, and if a peacock cried more than usual, then a death could be expected in the family.

In Japan, China and India among other countries, peacock feathers are considered good luck. The extra "eyes" are considered a positive force, offering protection. In India, they are said to ward off evil, and in Japan they are similarly considered a protective force. In Feng Shui, peacock feathers are a positive influence, offering protection, good luck, beauty and wealth. They are often placed around doorways and symbolize openness and vision.

THE FIRST THING YOU DO IN THE NEW YEAR

1st

New Year's Day is an important date in many cultures: the first fresh day of the new year ahead. Accordingly, many superstitions and traditions exist, centering specifically on the first thing you do on this significant day.

The identity of the first person to enter the house on New Year's Day is very important. In England, opinion was divided – it was generally accepted that a dark-haired individual was preferable, and that a light-haired visitor was bad luck, but in some locations the reverse was true, and it was a light-haired individual who should first cross the threshold. All were in agreement, however, that a female "first foot" was bad luck. Sometimes known as a "Lucky Bird", dark-haired boys would aim to be the first to enter, being rewarded with bread, cheese and money. In Renfrewshire, Scotland, the requirements were very specific – the first person to cross the threshold should be tall and dark, with feet that were not flat, and his eyebrows could not meet in the middle.

In Germany and Poland, eating herring as midnight strikes is thought to bring good luck for the year ahead. In Latvia, it is considered good luck to eat fish on New Year's Day, and putting the scales in your purse or wallet is said to mean money for the year ahead. In the southern US, a common dish eaten on New Year's Day is black eyed peas, mixed with greens and pork. The beans are said to bring good luck, especially for whoever finds the coin traditionally hidden in them.

In Poland, if you wake up early on the first day of the year, it is thought that you will do so every other day to come in the next 12 months. Some say that you should not wash clothes or dishes on New Year's Day, and others even caution against taking anything out of the house. According to Dutch belief, whatever you do on the first day of the year, you will be doing for the rest of the year. Choose your activity carefully!

INDEX

AUTHOR BIO

Willow Winsham is an author and historian specializing in witchcraft and folklore. She is the author of *Accused: British Witches Throughout History* and *England's Witchcraft Trials*, and co-author of *Treasury of Folklore: Seas and Rivers* and *Treasury of Folklore: Woodlands and Forests*. Willow is also co-founder of #folklorethursday, the popular website and Twitter account that shares fascinating stories and traditions from around the world.

Keep up with Willow on Twitter at @WillowWinsham and at her website www.willowwinsham.com

ACKNOWLEDGEMENTS

Writing this book has been a rollercoaster of a journey, and it would not have been possible without the help and support of a lot of very special people.

Firstly, a heartfelt thank you goes out to everyone on Twitter who has taken the time to answer my questions about superstitions over the last few months in an attempt to make this book as authentic as possible: you are too numerous to name, but I am grateful to each and every one of you!

I also need to thank my long suffering friends, both near and far, who have listened to me talk about all manner of weird and wonderful beliefs as I researched and wrote this book. I am deeply indebted to their suggestions and interest. A special shout out to Dee Dee Chainey for her constant moral and practical support throughout the writing of this book.

Lastly, a huge thank you to everyone at Welbeck and Sprung Sultan for their hard work and support throughout in making this book a reality.